# Acknowledgements

This book is dedicated to Ian Dunbar for his encouragement, his support, and his patience. It wouldn't exist without you, Ian!

I also want to acknowledge the most important people in my life: Nik, who encouraged me to pursue my dream of writing, and my parents, Dick and Ethel, who instilled in me the belief that I can do anything I desire. I love you!

Thanks to all my friends and colleagues who listened to me working out some of this material in my head and who read and commented on earlier versions. Thanks to Norma Nelson-Lomoro for managing to lay this all out while I continued to revise it!

And, finally, thanks to Shaahiin, Ciaran, and Eejit. You guys are so very, very special.

# Table of Contents

b

# *EXCEL*-ERATED LEARNING

Explaining in plain English how dogs learn and how best to teach them.

by
**Pamela J. Reid**
Ph.D.

*Excel*-erated Learning
by Pamela J. Reid

Drawings by Tascha Parkinson
Cover Design and Layout by Norma Nelson

First published February 1996

James & Kenneth Publishers
2140 Shattuck Avenue #2406
Berkeley, California 94704
(800) 784-5531

James & Kenneth - Canada
2353 Belyea Street
Oakville, Ontario L6l 1N8
(905) 469-1555 ext 3

James & Kenneth - UK
P O Box 111, Harpenden
Hertfordshire, AL5 2GD
01582 715765

© 1996 Pamela J. Reid

ISBN 1-888047-07-0

James & Kenneth
PUBLISHERS

# Forward

This book is written for people who teach dogs. The purpose is to make the reader understand the learning process so they can become better teachers and better trainers. It assumes a level of familiarity with obedience, agility, and flyball exercises that the average pet dog owner may not possess but my hope is that, for the most part, the information I have conveyed is accessible and useful to any person who works and/or lives with dogs.

For more information about this book and the material contained within it, contact:

James & Kenneth Publishers,
a division of the Center for Applied Animal Behavior,
2140 Shattuck Avenue #2406, Berkeley, CA 94704
or
Pamela J. Reid, Ph.D. at Pet Behaviour Innovations,
63 Vanevery Street, Toronto ON, Canada M8V 1Y5

# Introduction

As people who train dogs, we need to know a lot. We need to know how to handle dogs, how to observe and interpret their behavior, how to communicate with them, how to live with them, how to care for them, how to play with them, and how to teach them. Most trainers learn various methods for teaching. Few think about why these methods work or don't work in any given situation.

Almost everyone reading this book will know how to make a car operate: you can turn it on, make it move, make it stop, and so on. You might even be able to explain a bit about how a car is put together. But do you have the knowledge to fix the car if something goes wrong or if you want to change something it does? Most people would answer "no" - that stuff is left to the auto mechanic. And without this knowledge base, you would never say you truly understand cars. Yet if you really wanted to get into cars, you would expect to learn all about how the engine works, how the drive train works, how everything is connected, and so on.

That's the type of knowledge I'd like to provide you with, through this book. To really understand how a dog should be taught, you have to understand the underlying "machine"; the dog's equipment for learning. Then, not only can you determine how best to teach your dog something, you can also understand why some methods work and some don't for any particular behavior or any particular dog. With the freedom of understanding how your dog learns, comes the ability to make the learning process as easy as possible for your dog. Sure, there are many ways to teach, but some are more effective than others. Remember back in school - some of your teachers made learning very easy while others made learning a chore. You managed to get a grasp of the material no matter what but when the teacher put some thought into how to teach, it made learning so much easier. That's what you ought to be doing with your dog: making learning as easy and enjoyable as possible.

In this book, I explain the basic forms of learning and the underlying "rules" or laws which govern how learning occurs. It is amazing how powerful these laws of learning are. Basic conditioning can explain the vast majority of learning that occurs in all species, including humans. The only real difference in humans is that we can take shortcuts with language.

I focus on how learning theory and the laws of learning can be applied to the tasks faced by dog trainers. Presently, there are many, many different methods of training: click and treat, lure-reward, jerk and praise, motivational/drive training, shock collar training, and so on. They all, more or less, work within the basic laws of learning. Any training task can be analyzed in terms of what we want the dog to learn and what we want the final behavior to look like. The next question should be: what's the clearest, most efficient way to teach this to the dog? For one behavior, it might be click and treat, for another it might be lure-reward, and for another it might be training with a shock collar.

By providing you with the ability to understand how dogs learn, you will never be tied to any one technique. You will be able to decide what works best for your dog, as the learner, and what works best for you, as the teacher. You will be able to try different approaches to the same problem and develop new ones. You will never need to worry if you are doing a particular technique correctly because you will understand _why_ it works and therefore, _how_ it works. You'll be in a position to accelerate your dog's learning and therefore, excel in your training, hence: _excel_ - erated learning!

## A Few Comments About The Book

To make the book flow more easily, I have strayed from political correctness in favor of gender biases. Unless I am speaking of specific people and/or animals, I always refer to the animal as "he" and the human as "she". This is for no reason other than I am a "she" and each of my dogs is a "he". Also, sometimes I refer to "dog" and sometimes to "animal". The laws of learning hold up for all animals and people too. This isn't about how dogs learn, this is about how any living, breathing organism learns (well, provided it has a brain with more than a few neurons!).

If you are reading this and you happen to have earned a doctorate in learning theory, please don't be too rigid. There are many interpretations of a theory and I have provided the one I find most intuitive and easiest to grasp. Also, I might well say that something always works a certain way when there are exceptions. Unless the exceptions are particularly relevant, I will probably not tell you. So, for example, if 99% of all animals that have been studied learn something when you do x, y, and z but not when you add in q - I'll likely only tell you about x, y, and z. That is, unless dog training involves q's.

This is not a *how-to* book. This is a *why* book. And hopefully, it will be a book that will spark more creativity and independence in dog training. Animals, in general, and dogs, in particular, are fascinating creatures. Learning theory contains a great deal of information about the inner workings of animals and this information needs to get out to people, like you, who work with animals every day. We know a lot but there is always more to learn.

I often refer to my own dogs so I ought to introduce them. Sahraa'U Shaahiin Al BOrah, Am/Can CDX, FCh, FbCh, USDAA AD (Shaahiin) is my retired Saluki. Ciaran, Am CDX, FbCh, almost USDAA ADCH (22/23 legs), almost AAC MAD (5/6 legs) is my Border Collie. He's been a semi-finalist at the USDAA Grand Prix National event for the past five years and won the Open Jumping class two consecutive years. Eejit is an F1 hybrid: Border Collie x Border Terrier. He's still too young to compete in anything. I started out focusing on obedience but now I'm an avid agility competitor.

## What is Learning?

Psychologists have never really come up with a good definition of learning that everyone likes. Learning obviously involves some sort of change in behavior. Without a change in behavior, we would never be able to know if learning has occurred. But it must be a change in behavior that lasts awhile. You may have learned that when the telephone rings, you should pick it up but sometimes you may simply be too tired to get up and answer the phone. You haven't learned anything new - you're just too tired to show any behavior. You may have just talked on the telephone for an hour and you're totally unmotivated to spend any more time talking. Again, you haven't learned anything new - you just lack motivation. I'll come back to the topic of motivation in a later section. Learning also implies that whatever causes a change in behavior must have something to do with past experience. My puppy, Eejit, didn't used to jump for the Frisbee - he hadn't been provided the necessary experience. However, he also wasn't *able to* because he was too slow and uncoordinated physically. Now that he has matured, he can learn to play the game. Similarly, most trainers of young puppies forego teaching the straight sit in heel position because puppies tend to sit and flop over on one hip. Rather than teaching the puppy that a floppy sit is acceptable, the trainer waits until the puppy is sufficiently mature, physically, to perform the desired response: a straight sit.

## What is Learning Theory?

Learning theory is an explanation of how learning works; how learning comes to occur. All you can see is the behavior but if behavior changes, you assume that something has been learned. Learning is a process that occurs somewhere in the brain at some physical level. Your friend comes for a visit and offers to set up your new computer. You watch her go through the process. You *see* her going through the behaviors involved in setting up the computer but you *assume* that somehow, somewhere, she acquired the knowledge and skills to be able to do this. You assume that something happened in her brain that allowed her to acquire and retain this information. Learning theory attempts to explain how such changes occur - what has to happen in order for behavior to change?

## Knowing Versus Doing

Should you eat pizza for dinner tonight? That would probably depend on a number of factors, some of which might be: are you hungry? do you fancy pizza? what would you have to do to get pizza for dinner (pay money to have it made and delivered? make it yourself?), do you know the telephone number for a pizza delivery place? and so on. Only some of these factors involve learning. Others depend on motivation, available resources, etc.

This is the distinction between knowing something and doing something, called the *learning/performance distinction*. Whether or not a behavior is performed depends on a lot of things: opportunity, motivation, physical abilities, and learning. Consequently, just because a behavior does not occur, doesn't mean you can necessarily assume that the behavior has not been learned. Of course we have to depend on changes in behavior before we can assume learning has occurred but that does not rule out the possibility that learning has occurred without any change in behavior.

A laboratory example of learning without performance involved allowing a mouse to explore a complex maze. There was nothing in the maze of importance to the mouse and so the mouse wandered about, hither and thither. After a few days of letting the mouse explore, the experimenter put the mouse in a specific spot in the maze and gave him some cheese. She then removed the mouse before he had finished all the cheese and put him somewhere else in the maze. The mouse made a beeline through the maze back to the spot where the cheese was. It was obvious the mouse had learned the layout of the maze but he had no reason to display this learning before. This is called *latent learning*.

I am convinced, after raising my last two puppies, that both dogs had <u>learned</u> not to soil the house long before they were physically capable of controlling themselves to the point of getting to the correct place in time. They had acquired the knowledge but were still unable to perform in accord with this learning because they were insufficiently physically mature. That is the best way to explain the step-like nature of the house soiling. One day the puppy stopped having accidents and never looked back. However, there is absolutely no way I could ever verify this belief. Even if I were to open their brains and look inside, I couldn't point to any one spot and say "there, look, I knew this puppy had learned not to pee in the house!".

Always keep in mind that you are dealing with behavior and *inferring* learning.

## Motivation

As I have mentioned several times, motivation is one factor which influences whether or not a learned behavior will be performed. As trainers, we need to be well versed in the science of motivation as well as the science of learning theory because we can also manipulate the motivation of our animals. Motivation is like the gasoline in your car - without it, your car can't go anywhere. The car may be functioning perfectly but it needs "juice" to display it. Motivation is used to describe the forces which act on or within an animal to activate and direct behavior.

A concept that you may be familiar with is the drive theory of motivation. Several top trainers have adapted drive theory to explain why some dogs react to training differently. The idea behind drive theory is that each individual animal comes genetically "equipped" with varying levels of energy for different drives. My dog might possess a particularly strong "prey" drive, which means that he is highly likely to engage in predatory behavior at every opportunity and that he finds engaging in predatory behavior extremely reward-ing. Thus, my dog is highly motivated to reduce the need resulting from this drive state. According to drive theory, behavior is a result of both what has been learned and what is activated by the current drive level. If my dog is primarily activated by his hunger drive, he will engage in food-getting behaviors, particularly behaviors he has learned are related to obtaining food. If my dog is primarily activated by his prey drive, he will engage in predatory behaviors, such as stalking, chasing, biting, and so on. If my dog is activated by his "pack"drive, he will engage in social behaviors, such as nuzzling, grooming, etc.

In the psychological literature, drive theory as an explanation for motivation has gone out of fashion because few of the theoretical predictions were substantiated experimentally. It is useful, from a dog trainer's standpoint, as a mean for developing effective reinforcers for a specific dog and for identifying how a specific dog is likely to react to a given situation (in other words, what uncondi-tioned responses are likely to be elicited by a training scenario). Otherwise, I feel the theory's value is pretty limited.

The main point to understand is that the relationship between learning and motivation is so entwined that it is difficult to conceive of one without the other. For the most part, learning does not occur without motivation. Once a behavior has been learned, it may not be performed if the animal is not motivated to respond. In any training situation, you must consider the motivational state of the animal as well as the learning contingencies. You must also consider competing motivations. You may have a hungry dog that has acquired the response of coming when called in order to earn a food reward, but if the dog is loose and there are squirrels to be chased, you may not see the fruits of your training labours.

## The Four Stages of Learning

It is useful to think of learning as a sequence of four stages:

**1** acquisition (acquiring)

**2** fluency (automatic)

**3** generalization (application)

**4** maintenance (always)

The notion of the four A's (acquiring, automatic, application, always) is taken from a series of articles written by Marilyn Fender, Ph.D. and published in Front and Finish.

The acquisition stage is the first phase of learning, in which the animal acquires new knowledge. If you are teaching the dog to perform a trick, such as weaving through vertical poles in a slalom fashion, the dog must learn to maneuver in a certain manner through the obstacle in order to earn a reward. The dog has to learn what is expected of him and you, the trainer, focus on the accuracy of the response. Dr. Fender provides the example of a child learning the multiplication table. During the acquisition stage, the child must learn how to obtain the correct answer for each cell of the table.

The fluency stage is the second phase of learning in which the animal essentially becomes "fluent" in the new knowledge. When a dog is initially learning to weave, he has to methodically bend his body around each pole. Once he reaches the fluency stage, it is as though the behavior has become one fluid response - he develops a rhythm and it becomes automatic. Subjectively, the dog appears to have learned the behavior and now he can improve how cleanly and quickly he moves through the poles. During this phase of learning, the trainer can focus on enhancing the speed of the response. For the child learning the multiplication table, this is when the child can rapidly spit out accurate answers without even thinking.

The generalization stage is the phase of learning in which the animal learns that the new knowledge is relevant in a variety of circumstances and situations. The dog learning to weave must now learn that the weaving response can be applied in various situations. He can now be asked to perform the weaving response to a series of objects other than poles or to different sorts of poles, such as ones that stick in the ground versus ones on a base. He can be asked to perform the weaving response within a sequence of other behaviors. He can be asked to perform the weaving response to varying numbers of poles, rather than the usual 10 or 12. The child learning to multiply now learns to apply this knowledge to real-life situations, such as figuring out how many dog cookies to pack for 6 dogs going on a 12 day trip! Generalization is rarely automatic and special attention must be given to this phase of learning.

The maintenance stage is the phase of learning in which the animal incorporates the new knowledge into its behavioral repertoire. For the weaving dog, this means that the response of weaving is polished and reasonably consistent. When the dog hears the command "weave", he looks for a set of poles, enters correctly, and completes the sequence without breaking the flow. The trainer must continually ensure that the behavior is maintained at an acceptable level. For some dogs, this might require only an occasional training session in which weaving behavior is practiced. For other dogs, this might entail repetitions of exercises from previous stages, for instance, exercises to ensure accuracy, speed, or generalization of the response. In this stage, if the dog doesn't always perform the response, remedial action may be necessary. For the multiplying child, can she produce quick, accurate answers to multiplication questions a month later, a year later, even 10 years later?

# A Bit of History

## Why Study Animals?

The scientific study of how animals learn grew out of three different areas:

- some psychologists felt that understanding how animals learn would provide a "simple" model upon which to base the study of human learning.

- some psychologists were interested in the nervous system and how the brain physically changes as a result of learning. This pretty much had to be studied in animals because the researchers needed to "sacrifice" their subjects and look at brains.

- ethologists (biologists who are interested in the behavior of animals) began to recognize that much of the behavior they were studying was learned rather than "instinctive" (the preferred term is now "innate").

The study of animal learning is a very conservative and careful science, almost to the point of overkill. This is primarily because of the classification of psychology as a "soft" science. Psychology is the study of the mind but psychologists can't observe and measure the mind in the same way that a chemist can combine chemicals or that a physicist can measure the properties of objects. In their quest for scientific credibility, psychologists focused on developing experimental methods that rival any hard science. The following story will help you see why it was so important for the study of learning to be based on specific questions, carefully-designed experiments, and simple theories.

## The Story of Clever Hans

The story of Clever Hans is one of my favorites. Clever Hans was a horse that belonged to Wilhelm von Osten in Germany back in the early 1900s. Von Osten believed he had taught his horse to do math. He would write arithmetic problems on a chalk board and Clever Hans would tap out the answer with his hoof. If von Osten wrote: **5 + 3 =** Clever Hans would tap his foot against the floor 8 times.

The news of Clever Hans spread far and wide and eventually a group of scientists convened to study the horse. After watching a demonstration, they assigned a young student, Oskar Pfungst, to determine the extent of Hans's cleverness. Pfungst asked von Osten

and his horse to undergo a series of tests. Pfungst asked von Osten to read Hans the question rather than write it down, he blindfolded Hans and asked von Osten to read him the question, he asked von Osten to show Hans a card with the problem written on it, he asked von Osten to show Hans a card with a question on it that von Osten himself hadn't seen, and so on. Through this battery of tests, Pfungst discovered that Hans could only answer the problems correctly if von Osten knew the answer. If von Osten didn't know the answer, neither did Clever Hans. In other words, von Osten was somehow cuing the horse, whether intentionally or unintentionally.

It was Pfungst's task to find out how. It turned out that Hans could answer the questions correctly as long as he could see von Osten but if von Osten was hidden from view, either behind a wall or even standing outside the periphery of Hans's vision, Hans was unable to answer. Pfungst had other people in to ask questions of Hans and he still answered correctly. Pfungst began observing von Osten very carefully and finally he hit on it: whenever von Osten (or anyone else, for that matter) asked Hans a question, von Osten's eyebrows lowered as he watched Hans tap his foot. As he completed the correct number of taps, von Osten lifted his eyebrows.

Pfungst tested his theory himself. Without saying a word to Hans, he lowered his eyebrows and sure enough, Hans started tapping. Pfungst raised his eyebrows and Hans stopped tapping. Pfungst had solved the mystery of the clever horse!

The moral of the Clever Hans story is that things are not always what they seem. No matter how "obvious" something is, you never know for sure until you systematically rule out other explanations. And, in this case, a seemingly complex behavior had a very simple explanation. Caution was to become a cornerstone of the study of animal learning.

## The Principle of Parsimony

The **principle of parsimony** is a scientific principle which states that *unless there is evidence to the contrary*, you must account for a phenomenon with the simplest explanation available. C. Lloyd Morgan was the first to address the tendency of scientists to over interpret what animals do. He wrote what has come to be called Morgan's Canon:

"In no case is an animal activity to be interpreted in terms of higher psychological processes, if it can be fairly interpreted in terms of processes which stand lower in the scale of psychological evolution and development."

In other words, you can't assume that Hans had a concept of mathematics; you must assume the simplest explanation that can account for his behavior - that he was responding to minute, unintentional movements on the part of his trainer.

## The Science of Behaviorism

Before 1900, most accounts of learning in animals were anecdotal. People told amazing stories of wondrous intellectual feats by dogs, cats, horses, beavers, and so on. These stories were considered evidence that the mental activity we experience was shared by animals (although the abilities of the animals in these stories often rivaled the abilities of even gifted humans!).

However, the birth of *Behaviorism* provided an alternative to the anecdotal method. Behaviorism is the basis of a methodology that has permeated all areas of psychology for the past century. Behaviorism refers to the study of behavior, the study of observable events. For psychology to be considered a true science, a methodology had to be developed that would focus on something that could be observed, measured, and manipulated. That something is behavior. Proponents of behaviorism argued that behavior is lawful; that is, behavior follows certain rules; it is not random. Anything that is lawful can be objectively studied.

The acceptance of behaviorism went hand-in-hand with the rejection of the study of the mind. B. F. Skinner believed that we could understand behavior by studying the things that happen to animals. There was no need to study what was inside the animal's head. Understanding the laws of behavior and how events affect an animal's behavior do not necessitate understanding the mind. In fact, Skinner's form of *radical behaviorism* even rejected the notion that thoughts, feelings, and emotions could cause behavior. And so, the study of animal learning became a science in which experimenters manipulated specific events and looked to measure changes in behavior. No assumptions are made about what might or might not be changed inside the animal.

Fortunately, psychology has undergone a major shift in focus over the past 20 years or so and now it is acceptable to question what is going on inside the animal's head. Memory, problem solving skills, special abilities, and so on, are now considered acceptable areas of study. This shift has been called the "cognitive revolution". As yet, however, the science is in its infancy and offers little practical information to help us understand learning. Presumably this will change but for now, behaviorism will be the focus of this book.

# The Lingo

## Psychological Jargon

Jargon is the special language of a particular group or profession. Learning theory has been accused of having more jargon than any other field. Unfortunately, this means that it is extremely difficult for anyone to just pick up a book on learning theory and get through it without going mad!

The purpose of jargon is to use words that have very definite meanings. This is in contrast to our everyday words whose meanings often get muddied up. A good example is the word *reinforcer* rather than *reward*. A reinforcer is a reward but *reward* implies something that is considered to be good by the giver and hopefully by the recipient as well. *Reinforcer*, on the other hand, is very specific. A reinforcer is good because the recipient considers it good and because it serves as "pay", in that it makes the recipient do something to receive it. If the recipient doesn't do something to receive it, it is not considered a reinforcer. Throughout this book, I use the words *reinforcer* and *reward* interchangeably but I will always technically mean reinforcer.

Because my education and research background is in learning theory, the jargon is an integral part of my language and I do use it. Consequently, I will go through some of the more common terms that you will encounter in this book.

### Conditioning:

Conditioning means learning, plain and simple.

**Behavior/Response:**

Any action performed that can be observed and measured (i.e. walking, barking, lying down, pricking ears, etc.).

**Stimulus:**

Any event that can be perceived by the animal. A stimulus could be a light, a sound, a touch, a smell, etc.

**Consequence:**

An action or event (a stimulus) that occurs *after* a behavior. It may affect how often that behavior will occur in the future.

**Contingency:**

A statement of a dependent relationship between events. You can substitute "depends upon": whether my dog gets a cookie depends upon his sitting; getting a cookie is contingent upon sitting. You can substitute "if...then": if my dog lies down, then I'll throw the Frisbee; my throwing of the Frisbee is contingent upon his lying down.

**Performance:**

Performance refers to actual behavior - what you see is what you get. Just because an animal does not show a behavior, does not necessarily mean that learning has not taken place.

**Appetitive/Positive:**

Anything that the animal considers a good thing; anything that feels good, sounds good, tastes good, etc. (i.e. praising, Frisbee playing, tummy rubs, a good run, a soft bed, a game of tug, watching a squirrel, a quiet time in the sun, a dead groundhog to roll on or eat, on and on).

**Aversive/Negative:**

Anything that the animal considers a bad thing; anything unpleasant, painful, annoying, uncomfortable, etc. (i.e. shouting, hitting, ignoring, a leash jerk, ultrasonic sounds, quick movements, grabbing, restraining, shock, on and on).

**Theory/Principles**:

A theory is an explanation of how things work (i.e. learning theory is an account of how learning takes place) and principles are the rules outlined by the theory (i.e. learning principles are the rules or laws that govern learning; for instance, you wouldn't expect that you could teach a dog to sit by hitting him every time he sits - that would violate what we know about how learning works).

# Classical Conditioning

## What Goes with What?

Classical conditioning, Pavlovian conditioning, associative learning - these are all terms for what happens when an animal learns associations among things. Learning associations means learning that things go together: when one thing happens (you burn your dinner), another thing will follow shortly (the smoke detector goes off). You say "Let's go for a walk", your dog jumps up all excited because he has learned that this particular phrase precedes going out for a walk. Your cat runs to its food dish when it hears the can opener because often this signals feeding time. In each case, there is a predictable relationship among the events and the animal learns to respond to the first event *in anticipation* of the second event. That's what classical conditioning is all about: anticipation.

what's predictable in my world?

An excellent example of classical conditioning was provided by the founder himself: Ivan P. Pavlov. Pavlov was interested in how reflexes work and he studied the salivary reflex in dogs. Hungry dogs naturally salivate when presented with food. Quite by accident, Pavlov stumbled upon a major discovery. After a period of time in his experiments, Pavlov's dogs began to salivate as soon as they were brought into the experimental apparatus. And they salivated even more profusely when Pavlov's research technician, the person who actually presented the food, walked into the room. This was surprising for Pavlov because it meant that the dogs had come to associate the room and the technician with the experience of food and came to respond in the same way as they would to the food itself. The dogs were showing learned associations.

Pavlov then tried to associate various stimuli with the delivery of food: bells, buzzers, tones, music, metronomes, visual patterns, rotating objects, a touch. At first none of these stimuli would cause a dog to salivate but if one was consistently presented for a few seconds prior to the presentation of food, the stimulus would eventually produce copious salivation by itself. The dog would even try to approach the stimulus, licking his lips. In Pavlov's words: "the animal reacts to the signal in the same way as if it were food; no distinction can be observed between the effects produced on the animal by the sounds of the beating metronome and showing it real food" (Pavlov, 1927, p.22).

Pavlov's experiments embody the basics of associative learning. An initially neutral or meaningless stimulus (the *conditioned stimulus* or CS) is presented prior to the delivery of an *unconditioned stimulus* or UCS. The UCS is unconditioned because presentation of the UCS always elicits an *unconditioned response* or UCR. For instance, food always elicits salivation. The dog doesn't have to learn to salivate when eating - it just happens. Once the animal has learned the association between the neutral stimulus and the unconditioned stimulus, the neutral stimulus itself elicits a response, which is called the *conditioned response* or CR. It looks better than it reads:

**At first:** **CS (tone)** → **UCS (food)**
↘ **UCR (salivates)**

**After learning:** **CS (tone)** → **UCS (food)**
↘ **CR (salivates)** ↘ **UCR (salivates)**

I want to point out that there is nothing about this arrangement that *requires* the animal to perform the conditioned response. The dog doesn't need to salivate when the tone comes on. The food (the UCS) is delivered no matter what the animal does. The CR just happens; it's involuntary. It happens because the animal has learned that when one thing happens, another thing is likely to happen. If that other thing is relevant to the animal, you see a response to the first thing in anticipation of the second.

If you think classical conditioning only affects simple behaviors, like salivating, think again. When you throw the dumbbell, you're very likely to send your dog to get it. After a few of these, the dog starts to anticipate and leaves right after you throw it. This is classical conditioning.

---

## At-Home Experiment

See if you can classically condition a friend to blink her eye when she hears a specific noise. For this experiment, you need two chairs (placed with the backs facing each other), a subject (your friend), a device which makes a noise (such as a pen that clicks or a timer that beeps), and a drinking straw. You straddle one chair with your head resting on your hands, elbows placed on the back of the chair. Your friend straddles the other, facing you with her head resting on her hands. You position the straw by your mouth and directed at her eye (no eyeglasses are permitted). Blow a quick puff of air through the straw. This should cause her to blink (try not to spit through the straw!). Now you are ready to begin. Every 5-10 seconds, sound your noisemaker (a very quick noise) and almost immediately blow through the straw. Repeat this approximately 20 times. Then conduct a test trial: make the noise but don't blow. Did she blink in anticipation? If not, perform another 20 or so trials before attempting a test.

In order to classically condition a *reliable* eyeblink, you would have to go through the pairing as many as a few hundred times, and if you were to do that, your friend would involuntarily blink whenever she heard a pen click! **Different behaviors condition at different rates.** Eyeblink conditioning is an easy procedure to set up but it doesn't condition easily. Other behaviors, such as salivating, take relatively few pairings for reliable conditioning.

I had the bizarre experience of developing a conditioned response in myself a while back. I was frequently competing at agility events and my friend would record several runs throughout the weekend. The next week we would sit and analyze the videos. One of the nice things about the sport of agility is that everyone applauds each run. *While watching the videos,* I realized that I was clapping at the end of each run! I was very embarrassed but I found it extremely difficult not to clap. I had to really concentrate on resisting the urge. The events surrounding the end of a run (the CSs: the handler and dog running faster, the handler's arms going up in the air, the dog jumping up on the handler, etc.) had become associated with the excitement of watching a real run (the UCS), which is followed by applause. It was very strange!

Associative conditioning can be used to train dogs to perform behaviors that are difficult to induce the dog to do, such as sneezing, growling, snarling, digging, and the like. The most efficient strategy is to identify a stimulus that reliably elicits the behavior and then precede that stimulus with a neutral stimulus such as a spoken command. If Eejit wants me to kick snow or leaves for him and I refuse, he becomes very frustrated and starts to whine and dig at my feet. I used this to teach him to dig on command. I started by saying "dig", then I moved my feet but did not kick anything. This caused him to begin digging. After a few pairings, he digs on command!

If tickling your dog's nose with a feather causes him to sneeze, then you can say "Sneeze!" and then reach forward to tickle him with the feather so that he sneezes. With sufficient pairings, he should sneeze when you say the word, because he has learned the association between the word and the feather. Of course, in both of these examples, the dog learns the behavior even more quickly if you also reward him for the behavior - but that's the next section.

# Operant Conditioning

## Does What I Do Affect What Happens to Me?

Operant conditioning, instrumental learning[1], Skinnerian conditioning - these are all terms for what happens when an animal learns that its behavior has consequences. Learning that a particular behavior has a consequence might be as simple as learning that rolling over on your side in bed feels good or as complex as learning that solving difficult mathematical problems leads to an opportunity to receive a scholarship. There are countless things we do everyday that lead to consequences that wouldn't happen if we hadn't done something. If you don't work, you don't get paid. If you don't cook, you don't eat. If I ask my dog to sit and he doesn't, he doesn't get a treat. If he were a wild animal and he didn't bother to go out and hunt, he wouldn't eat. In other words, things happen because we do things and animals learn these relationships the same as do people.

How does my behavior affect what happens to me?

_____

[1] It is called operant conditioning because the behavior operates on, or has an effect on, the animal's world. It is also called instrumental conditioning: responses occur because they are instrumental in making something happen.

The process of operant conditioning is displayed in this formula:

$$S^D \rightarrow R \rightarrow S$$

The $S^D$ stands for *discriminative stimulus*. This might be your command or cue for your dog to perform a specific behavior. The R refers to *response* and this could be any response your dog is capable of

# Thorndike's Law of Effect:

doing. This response leads to a consequence or *stimulus*. The observation that the consequences of a behavior determine whether the behavior will occur again led Thorndike to propose the *Law of Effect*:

*If a consequence is pleasant, the preceding behavior becomes more likely. If a consequence is unpleasant, the preceding behavior becomes less likely.*

Another popular way to remember this process is to think of it as the ABC's of learning:

## Antecedent → Behavior → Consequence

The antecedent stimulus is the discriminative stimulus, the behavior is the response, and the consequence is the stimulus that occurs as a result of the behavior. Instrumental conditioning is very different from classical conditioning in that the animal must perform a behavior in order for the stimulus to be presented. Aside from the $S^D$, the events that occur are under the animal's control.

## The Four Possibilities

In the operant sequence, there are four possible scenarios, two of which *increase* the likelihood that the behavior will occur again and two of which *decrease* the likelihood that the behavior will occur again.

### Positive Reinforcement

Positive reinforcement involves the presentation of a good consequence when the response is performed. For instance, you say "sit" (the $S^D$), your dog sits (the R), and you give him a treat (the $S^{R+}$). This serves to **increase** the likelihood of the response in the future. Much of dog training is based on methods that incorporate positive reinforcement. Human behavior is also regulated by positive reinforcement: child does homework, child is awarded good grade; child does chores, child is given allowance; person works hard for several months, person goes on holiday; I write a section of this book, I visit the Belgian chocolate shop!

### Negative Reinforcement

Negative reinforcement involves the removal of a bad consequence when the response is performed. For instance, you say "sit" (the $S^D$), your dog sits (the R), and you stop choking him with a noose collar (the $S^{R-}$). This also serves to **increase** the likelihood of the response in the future. Negative reinforcement is also a common method for controlling behavior: child does homework to avoid mom's nagging, person bangs on the ceiling to complain about the noise upstairs, Nik works late to escape having to take the dogs out on a rainy evening, Eejit doesn't stray off the sidewalk to avoid my shouting at him, I travel to the university each day to write so I can avoid telephone calls.

## Positive Punishment

Positive punishment involves the presentation of a bad consequence when the response is performed. For instance, you say "sit" (the $S^D$), your dog lies down (the R), and you jerk him onto his feet with the leash (the $P^+$). This serves to **decrease** the likelihood of the response in the future. We see positive punishment a lot: child hits brother, father spanks child; person drives after drinking, person ends up in the slammer; puppy pees on the floor, puppy gets hit with a rolled-up newspaper; I stop paying attention for a second and a dog bites me.

## Negative Punishment

Negative punishment involves the removal of a good consequence when the response is performed. For instance, you say "sit" (the $S^D$), your dog lies down (the R), and you eat the treat you were just about to pop into his mouth (the $P^-$). This also serves to **decrease** the likelihood of the response in the future. Child swears at table, TV turned off that evening; person drives after drinking, person loses license; I speak rudely to someone on the telephone, they refuse to hire me; Eejit plays too rough, I walk away.

This is called a contingency table:

| | | ACTION | |
| | | Present | Take away |
|---|---|---|---|
| **STIMULUS** | **Good** | **Positive Reinforcement** Present something good: behavior is more likely. | **Negative Punishment** Take away something good: behavior is less likely. |
| | **Bad** | **Positive Punishment** Present something bad: behavior is less likely. | **Negative Reinforcement:** Take away something bad: behavior is more likely. |

As you can see, the stimulus that follows a behavior can be good or bad and the contingency (relationship) between the behavior and the stimulus can be positive or negative (you can present something or take something away, conditional upon the behavior). Positive and negative reinforcement are both good, as far as the *dog* is concerned, and so the response is more likely to occur again. Positive and negative punishment are both bad, as far as the *dog* is concerned, and so the response is less likely to occur again. Positive reinforcement and positive punishment are both good, as far as most *trainers* are concerned, because both procedures involve the use of positive stimuli. Negative reinforcement and negative punishment are both bad, as far as most *trainers* are concerned, because both procedures involve the use of negative stimuli. Dog trainers, however, do usually incorporate all four of these processes when teaching people and animals.

---

**Remember:**

Reinforcement, whether positive or negative, causes the behavior to be more likely.

Punishment, whether positive or negative, causes the behavior to be less likely.

---

## Classical or Operant Behavior?

In the psychological laboratory, black and white distinctions can be made between classical and operant conditioning. Classically conditioned responses occur even though nothing is required of the animal: the UCS is presented no matter what the animal does. Operant responses occur because the situation is set up such that if the animal performs the response, something happens and if he doesn't, something doesn't happen (or vice versa). With operant conditioning, what the animal does is critical to what happens next.

In the real world, it is usually not meaningful to ask whether classical or operant conditioning is in operation because things aren't that clear-cut. Both types of learning play a critical role in any situation. Some of the learning will involve associations between stimuli (classical) and relationships between stimuli, responses, and consequences (operant). Even though picking up your dog's leash may elicit classically conditioned feelings of excitement and anticipation in your dog which cause him to come running, the behavior of coming is rewarded with a walk (operant conditioning). Even though the sound of the tin opener causes your cat to salivate and feel hungry (classical conditioning), he comes running into the kitchen because often running into the kitchen is rewarded with dinner (operant conditioning).

Here's an example of the distinction between classical and operant conditioning. Suppose you love pizza and you haven't eaten for 24 hours. Your friend orders a pizza with all your favorite ingredients. Then your friend offers you $100 **not** to eat any of the pizza. You want the $100 more than the pizza so you choose not to eat. The response of picking up the pizza and putting it in your mouth is an example of instrumental conditioning. The behavior can be thought of as voluntary (emitted) and so you can choose to inhibit this response. However, no matter how much money your friend offers you, you would not be able to suppress the behavior of salivating when you see and smell the pizza. This is because salivating to the sight and smell of the pizza (visual and olfactory stimuli which have been associated with eating pizza) are classically conditioned responses. These behaviors can be thought of as involuntary or reflexive (elicited)[2].

---

[2] This is a bit simplified. It is believed that an association is established between the CS and a mental representation of the UCS. The conditioned response is not truly involuntary because if the thought of the UCS is no longer a good thing (if you'd had a pizza for breakfast, lunch, and dinner for the past week), then you won't display a conditioned response on this particular occasion (you won't salivate).

However, if the two types of learning are at odds with each other, I'd place my bet on the classically conditioned response as having the major impact on behavior. Here's why: Marian and Keller Breland were associates of B.F. Skinner and studied operant conditioning for several years. They decided to break out on their own in the business world, establishing a company called *Animal Behavior Enterprises* for the purpose of training animals for television, films, displays at fairs and amusement parks. Until the Brelands trained a variety of different species to perform many different responses, it was believed that any animal could be conditioned to perform any response, given the physical ability to do so. In fact, Skinner once claimed that, with the right reinforcement contingencies, a cow could be trained to stalk and pounce on "an animated bundle of corn" (Skinner, 1977, p. 1011). The Brelands found that things were not quite that simple. They began to experience breakdowns in the performance of their animals. In 1961, they published an article with the title *"The Misbehavior of Organisms"*: a parody of the title of Skinner's first major work *"The Behavior of Organisms"* (1938). In the words of the Brelands:

> We started out by reinforcing |the raccoon| for picking up a single coin. Then the metal container was introduced, with the requirement that he drop the coin into the container. Here we ran into the first bit of difficulty: he seemed to have a great deal of trouble letting go of the coin. He would rub it up against the inside of the container, pull it back out, and clutch it firmly for several seconds. However, he would finally turn it loose and receive his food reinforcement. Then the final contingency: we |required| that he pick up |two| coins and put them in the container.

> Now the raccoon really had problems (and so did we). Not only could he not let go of the coins, but he spent seconds, even minutes, rubbing them together (in a most miserly fashion), and dipping them into the container. He

carried on this behavior to such an extent that the practical application we had in mind - a display featuring a raccoon putting money into a piggy bank - simply was not feasible. The rubbing behavior became worse and worse as time went on, in spite of nonreinforcement.

The Brelands had similar difficulties with other species. Pigs also could not be conditioned to put coins into a piggy bank. After the initial training, on the way to the bank, the pig would repeatedly drop the coin, pick it up, root it along the ground, toss it in the air, and so on. A chicken was trained to use a bat to hit a "baseball", with the stipulation that the ball had to hit the rear wall in order for the chicken to be reinforced. After a time, the chicken began chasing the ball and pecking at it, thus preventing it from reaching the wall. At first, the Brelands assumed the animals were not sufficiently motivated so they further deprived them of food. This actually intensified the behaviors.

What was really happening was that the animal was forming a classically conditioned association between the signal for food (the coins or the ball) and the delivery of the food itself. The CS was the coin and the UCS was the food. And so the "misbehaviors" reported by the Brelands were actually classically conditioned responses (feeding-related behaviors) directed toward the CS. When classical and operant behaviors are at odds with each other, the classically conditioned response interferes with, and can even override, the operant response.

The majority of dog training consists of operant conditioning so this will be a major focus of the remainder of the book. However, I often come back to classical conditioning because if you don't understand how it works, you can end up incorporating procedures that interfere with what you are trying to accomplish. You can be in for an extremely difficult time if you try to teach a behavior that is incompatible with the behaviors that are elicited by reinforcement. I came across a study in which the experimenter trained dogs to pick up a ball and deposit it into a container in order to activate the feeder. Very similar to the racoon story, except that the dogs were able to learn this task. The experimenter noted that the first indication that the dogs were learning anything came in the form of the dogs pricking up their ears and staring at the feeder. However, *none* of the dogs were able to learn the task until this anticipation response disappeared. It disappeared because as long as they stood and stared at the feeder, the feeder didn't work (sort of like watching a kettle boil). Eventually, they gave up staring at the feeder and were able to focus on learning the task at hand. If the experimenter had required the dogs to pick up the feeder and drop it in the container, the dogs would have been faced with the same conflict as the racoons!

You also may find that, during the course of training or perfecting a behavior, your dog may display behaviors that interfere with what you are trying to achieve. If you can identify these behaviors as classically conditioned responses, you will be in a better position to know how to alter the situation. For instance, you might be trying to get your dog to perform agility at a local fair but the stimuli associated with the fair elicit conditioned fear in the dog and this, then, interferes with the dog's performance. Especially if you are involved in trying to rehabilitate problem dogs, classical conditioning must be a major component of your bag of tricks.

# Single-Event Learning

## What's Important in My World?

The last type of learning I want to describe is called single-event learning. This form of learning is actually the simplest, most basic example of learning. A single event means something that happens (a stimulus) that is not related to anything else. There are many things, especially noises and movements, that will initially cause a dog notice, maybe even startle. If someone were to walk into the room right now, you would probably turn toward the stimulus. This is called an *orienting response*. However, many things are not important enough to warrant a response and so if the thing occurs a number of times, we come to ignore it as part of the background. For instance, a young dog often reacts to noises from the TV, such as barking dogs, doorbells, etc. However, after a time, he learns to ignore these noises because they never have any relevance to him. A dog that lives in an apartment building learns that the sounds of people coming and going outside the door are irrelevant (unless the noises stop at his door) and so stops barking at every hallway sound. If you were to ring a bell occasionally for no good reason, your dog would still learn something about that stimulus. If the bell was unrelated to anything of significance to your dog, he would cease reacting. The ability to stop reacting to meaningless stimuli is called *habituation*. Anything that occurs over and over again may lead to habituation.

The next time you encounter a snail, try this experiment. Blow on the snail and it will pop into its shell. It will probably take a good while to come back out again. Eventually it will. Blow on it again. In it goes. This time it may come out a second or two sooner. Blow on it again. Eventually, the snail will pop into its shell when you blow on it but then it will come back out almost immediately. If you continue, eventually the snail will not even bother to react to the puff of air at all. The snail has learned that this particular stimulus - the puff of air - has no relevance and therefore, habituates to it. It ceases responding. This is learning that makes good sense. Imagine what life would be like for snails if they retreated into their shells for every puff of breeze!

There are two types of habituation: one that occurs over the course of a few repetitions of the stimulus within a short time period and one that takes much longer. For instance, a dog will startle if keys are dropped on the floor but will habituate quickly if this happens repeatedly over the next few minutes. However, hours or days later, the dropped keys will once again elicit a startle response. This return of responding is called *spontaneous recovery*. Only after many sessions will long-term habituation to the dropped keys occur.

Short-term habituation occurs more readily if the repetitions occur at short intervals, for instance, every few seconds. If you drop your keys every few seconds for a couple of hours, your dog will very quickly stop reacting. If you then take a break for a couple of hours and then drop your keys again, your dog will likely react again. The short time interval between repetitions enhances short-term habituation. However, if you drop your keys say, once an hour, over an entire day, it will take longer for your dog to stop reacting. If you then take a break the next day and on Day 3 you drop your keys again, you will get less spontaneous recovery of the reaction because the long intervals between repetitions enhances long-term habituation.

Although this may sound extremely bizarre to you, there is some evidence to suggest that animals actually habituate to a reward. If you always use the same type of reinforcer during training and the dog experiences a number of rewards in a row, even though the dog may still be very hungry, responses will become less vigorous simply because he is habituating to the same old reward. Use various types of rewards in your training to avoid this strange decrease in your dog's enthusiasm.

## Sensitization

A loud noise, such as a gun, may startle your dog at first but if you continue to repeat it over and over, some dogs will habituate to the noise. Notice that I said "some", rather than "all", because of a phenomenon called *sensitization*. Sensitization is sort of the opposite of habituation. Instead of habituating to a repeated stimulus, sometimes the animal will sensitize to it: his reaction becomes even stronger. A good example of this is a dog that fears thunder. Taking a trip to the jungle during the rainy season usually won't work to eliminate a dog's fear of thunder! Likewise, spending a Sunday at the local firing range won't necessarily alleviate your dog's fear of gunfire. Instead, the dog's reaction may become even more extreme.

Stimuli that elicit really strong emotional reactions, such as fear, often don't habituate. Instead they continue to affect the general arousal of the animal and make the response even stronger. Think of how you feel after seeing a really scary horror flick - every little noise or movement makes you startle. That's sensitization at work. Sensitization is actually quite different from habituation because it is more general. Habituation is very specific. A dog that has habituated to a particular sound will definitely still react to other noises.

Sensitization, however, is not stimulus specific at all. A sensitized dog will over-react to all sorts of things. During a thunderstorm, your fearful dog may flinch at any novel sound, touch, or movement. The dog is generally more aroused about everything.

### Habituation or Sensitization?

It is sometimes difficult to predict whether repeated presentations of a stimulus will produce habituation or sensitization. In general, really intense stimuli often lead to sensitization while weak stimuli usually habituate. However, individual differences also play a role. One study looked at the ability of kittens to habituate to the presence of a dog nearby. A quiet, calm dog was brought into the room where the cats were housed, several times a day for a minute each time (with a minute in between each time). At first, these kittens reacted with threat displays: arching the back, crouching, growling, hissing, spitting, swatting. Over time, a few of the kittens habituated quickly. However, others sensitized and their threat displays became even more intense as the experience was repeated. More interesting, some kittens started out by sensitizing and eventually habituated while others initially showed

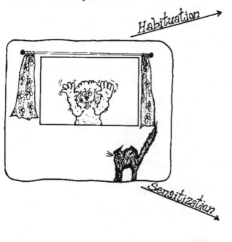

habituation but then began to sensitize! The difference between habituation and sensitization was very obvious in this situation. When a new dog was brought into the kittens' room, the kittens that had shown habituation to the former dog showed threat displays again. However, the kittens that had sensitized to the dog were ready to attack anything presented to them, including the experimenter! None of these kittens had any experience, good or bad, with dogs before the experiment.

The first time I sounded an ultrasonic device (a Pet Agree), Shaahiin looked at me curiously and Ciaran darted away, tail tucked, to hide under the bed. Out of curiosity, I sounded it a couple of times at my weekly classes to see how many dogs would show each type of response. Of course, Shaahiin and Ciaran were always present at these classes. After maybe 10-20 experiences, Ciaran had totally habituated to the sound and hardly even blinked an eye, while Shaahiin had sensitized and would get terribly upset and try to leave the room.

## Adaptation

I sometimes hear habituation and adaptation used interchangeably. Adaptation is quite different because it does not involve learning. Adaptation refers to the physical process of tiring. Perceiving a stimulus requires that the animal uses its senses. The sensory neurons can tire and when they do, they actually stop working. Think of what happens when you look directly at a flash bulb firing. You see a spot of white for some time. That's because your visual neurons have been fried and temporarily stop working. That's sensory adaptation and it can also happen if you simply repeatedly show the same stimulus over and over and sound the same stimulus over and over. Sensory adaptation is of great concern to handlers of detection dogs because it is not known how much olfactory stimulation leads to adaptation. Motor adaptation is similiar but it involves tiring of the motor neurons that command the muscles to work. When habituation is at work, the animal is still able to perceive the stimulus and it is still able to make the response. It doesn't react, however, because it has learned not to.

## Learned Irrelevance

There is a phenomenon called learned irrelevance that is very similar to habituation. Imagine that you have two dogs that you want to train to come when called. One dog has heard the command "come" many times before because he is crated near a training area and people frequently practice recalls with their dogs next to his crate. So the dog has heard the command "come" in the past but it has had no meaning for him because there has been no consequence. The other dog was housed in another building and has never heard the "come" command before. Now you begin training the dogs to come for food when they hear the command. You will discover that the dog who heard the command before learns much more slowly than the dog who had never heard the command before. That's because the dog who had heard the command many times before learned the irrelevance of the command and so doesn't even pay attention to it when you use it during training[3]. The other dog never heard the word before and so he attends to it. Thus, it is easier for him to learn that the command is now a signal for food. An animal that ceases attending to a stimulus because it has no consequence is displaying *learned irrelevance* (it is also known as the pre-exposure effect) and this results in slower learning if the stimulus is then incorporated into a training sequence. Learned irrelevance is very efficient. Animals should learn to ignore things that are of no importance to them and to attend to stimuli that are.

Think about what many pet owners do with their dogs *before* you

---

[3] This is not the same as the puppy who learns to respond to "come" by following an older dog who has been trained to the command. This is more likely social facilitation and we will discuss this form of learning in a later section.

ever see them in a training class. Often, the owner will use a certain command, such as "come", without ever teaching the dog what is expected of him. Thus, it is highly likely that the dog has heard the word many, many times with no consequence. The dog has learned the irrelevance of the word and it will be more difficult to teach the dog to come to the command "come" than if you change to a new word the dog has rarely or never heard before. So if you think the dog has heard a command a zillion times before, you would be better off to switch to a new word before beginning training.

An common example of learned irrelevance is the ringing of the telephone. Most dogs learn the irrelevance of the telephone ringing[4]. It typically has no consequence one way or the other for a dog. Thus, the dog learns to tune out the ringing of the telephone.

Learned irrelevance seems, at first glance, to be much like habituation. The dog stops reacting to a stimulus which is repeated over and over again and nothing else happens. However, the two phenomena are different because learned irrelevance is not susceptible to spontaneous recovery. A response that has habituated recovers after an interval of time has passed without experiencing the stimulus. A stimulus that is irrelevant to the dog will be more difficult to condition at a later date even if a substantial amount of time has passed between the exposure and the conditioning.

With dogs that go ballistic when the doorbell rings, I used to recommend teaching the dog the irrelevance of the doorbell. I would tell the owner to ring the doorbell a lot. Ideally, she would rig up something so she can ring it while inside. If it happens enough, the dog will eventually learn that more often than not, when the doorbell rings, either no one bothers to get up and do anything or if they

---

[4] This actually may not be a great example. It's not uncommon to receive a telephone call from frantic, harried dog owner that spends more time shouting at the dog than talking to me. I suspect that the dog **has** learned something about the telephone ringing: that the owner is occupied and unable to monitor the dog's activities. These dogs display this learning by barking and biting at the helpless owner, running off to get into the garbage, or some other misbehavior!

do get up and open the door, no one is there. The owner needs to ring the bell surreptitiously so the dog does not learn to tell which rings are meaningless and which are real. Because there is no consequence for the dog (no guest to make a fuss over him), he should eventually stop reacting when the doorbell rings. However. in order for this to work, the number of meaningless rings has to far exceed the number of "real" rings.

I have to admit that I stopped recommending this procedure when I tried it with Eejit and discovered how difficult it is. It seemed as though Eejit became sensitized by the doorbell and his barking actually escalated for a time. After a solid hour of ringing the doorbell every 30 seconds, he eventually ceased barking but was still very alert. After a break of only 20 minutes, Eejit's barking returned at full volume!

Treating a dog suffering from separation anxiety provides another example of teaching the irrelevance of certain conditioned stimuli. Most dogs that suffer from separation anxiety become agitated and aroused while the owner is getting ready to leave. Treatment is facilitated if the owner actively engages in these activities without leaving and not always engaging in these activities when she does go out. Under these conditions, the dog is unable to predict when the owner is going out and when she is staying home and so cannot become anxious in anticipation of being left alone.

# Factors That Affect Learning

Now that you are familiar with the three basic forms of learning, I want to explore how different factors affect learning. Learning can be affected in terms of how quickly or how thoroughly a response is acquired (the acquisition and fluency stages) and how easily or how long a response is retained (the generalization and maintenance stages). You can use any or all of these factors to help you influence the rate and extent of your dog's learning.

## Deprivation Level

It shouldn't surprise you to learn that a hungry animal works harder for food; a thirsty animal works harder for water; a rested animal works harder for play; an isolated animal works harder for social interaction. In rat-running studies, the hungrier the rats, the faster they run to get to the goal box. This is directly applicable to dogs, provided the response you are

asking for is simple, like running a maze. If you are requiring a complex set of responses, sometimes intense motivation can work against you. The dog becomes so distracted by the anticipation of the reward that his responding becomes sloppy and erratic. (Remember the section on the conflict between classical and operant behaviors.)

Deprivation is the reason why some trainers recommend crating a dog for a time before and after a training session. If the dog is particularly motivated by social attention, crating the dog before training will produce a dog that is deprived of this reward. Crating the dog <u>after</u> training as well will make the discrimination that it is *training* that is associated with the reward clearer to the dog. The idea is that the dog never gets social interaction for "free", just like I prefer that my dogs never get Rollover for free. Crating as a means of deprivation is not something that I recommend to pet owners because I doubt many would actually comply. I, myself, would have a hard time of it. Food deprivation is more acceptable to most people. I believe it is much easier to ask pet owners to train just before a meal, so that at least the hunger level of the dog is at its peak.

Here's an interesting thing about deprivation. Imagine you have two groups of dogs: one group is mildly hungry, the other group is extremely hungry. The extremely hungry group will learn to run down an alley to get to food more quickly than the mildly hungry group. After extensive training under these conditions, you can increase the amount of food given to the extremely hungry dogs such that they are only mildly hungry and *they will continue to run faster* than the group of dogs that were mildly hungry all along.

If you are training a behavior that requires intense, fast responding, make sure your dog is well-deprived of whatever reinforcement you are using. Then, once he has learned the behavior, you can decrease the level of deprivation without decreasing the intensity of his response.

With classical conditioning, an increase in deprivation level also leads to more rapid learning because this makes the UCS more salient or noticeable to the animal. A hungry dog is more likely to notice a piece of food than is a stuffed dog. Anything that makes the

UCS more salient results in better conditioning.

## The Reward

The amount and the quality of the reward (the palatability) have direct effects on behavior: animals work harder for larger or more tasty rewards. Also, if given a choice, animals prefer several small bits of food to one big bit of food, even if they both add up to the same amount. This is because the act of engaging in eating is itself very rewarding.

Conducting preference tests with dogs is a difficult proposition. If you were to sit down and show your dog a variety of different food treats and then allow him to make a choice, he'd probably grab whatever is closest, biggest, smelliest, or whatever he was last shown. That's because dogs are unable to show any self-control when food is involved. That's goes for all animal and small children as well. They grab something without taking time to contemplate the choice.

There was one nifty study in which a chimp was shown two different amounts of food, say 5 peanuts and 3 peanuts, and was asked which should be given to another chimp in the room. The other would be left for her. She always, always chose the larger amount first, even though she had to then watch the other chimp eat it. There was no doubt that she was able to understand the task, though, because this chimp had been trained to understood numbers. If the experimenter put numbers down instead of the actual food (the symbols 3 and 5), the chimp always, always chose the smaller number first. She understood the rules of the game but was unable to control herself to the point of pointing at the smaller amount of food.

## Contrast Effects, Jackpots, and Reinforcer Sampling

If an animal expects a particular reward and gets something else, you ought to see his behavior change. For instance, a good reward is considered really excellent if the animal has just experienced a mediocre one, and likewise, a mediocre reward is considered pretty dismal if the animal has just had a good one. So if you normally use wieners for treats and suddenly one day, you present a piece of chicken liver, your dog ought to be thrilled and try even harder to get the goodies (this is called *positive behavioral contrast*). If you normally use liver but one day you discover you're all out and have to use your dog's regular kibble, don't expect a resounding performance from your dog (this is called *negative behavioral contrast*)!

We know this from research with mice running mazes. The indication of learning for maze-running is usually the speed with which the mouse reaches the goal box from the start box. If the hungry mouse always finds a piece of mouse kibble in the goal box (a decent reward for a hungry mouse but not terribly thrilling) and then one day discovers a piece of Stilton cheese in the goal box, the next time he's given an opportunity to run the maze, he does so much more quickly than before. On the other hand, if the mouse is normally accustomed to finding Stilton cheese and one day there is only a piece of mouse kibble, the next time he'll run the maze much more slowly than before.

However, it's not just as simple as running hard for Stilton and not running so hard for kibble. The mouse that is accustomed to finding kibble but then finds Stilton actually runs *faster* than the mouse that always runs for Stilton. And the mouse that is accustomed to Stilton but then finds kibble actually runs *slower* than the mouse that always runs for kibble. In other words, to the Stilton-eating mouse, kibble is even more dreary than it is for the mouse that gets it all the time and to the kibble-eating mouse, Stilton is

totally amazing, much more so than it is for the mouse that gets it all the time.

This makes sense, really, because we all know that something we get very rarely is considered very special and that is always in relation to what we are accustomed to. However, the contrast effect is quite transient and usually only lasts for 1-2 trials after the discrepant reward. This relates directly to the use of *jackpots* or "rewards for excellence" in training. Jackpots are an attempt to capitalize on positive contrast by providing a special reward for a really excellent response. It might be a qualitatively different reward than the usual fare, such as Stilton instead of kibble, or it might be quantitatively different, such as presenting a whole handful of kibble. This is based on the notion that providing a special reward for a particularly well-performed response will somehow increase the likelihood of excellent responses in the future. Unfortunately, I don't know of any research that addresses that issue directly. It is true that an especially salient reinforcer has a greater effect on learning than a not-so-salient one but whether an occasional jackpot makes any noticeable difference is unclear, scientifically speaking. However, we do know that jackpots can serve to energize and motivate the dog's next response, through positive contrast. There is also no evidence to suggest that qualitatively different rewards are more or less superior to quantitatively different rewards.

Bear in mind that the term jackpot refers to a reward for excellence, not as a noncontingent reward to motivate the dog. I have heard trainers use jackpot to refer to the latter procedure as well. If the extra special reward is given in a specific context but is not related to the quality of the response, this would more appropriately be termed counter conditioning (this is covered in a later section). For example, if your dog is not keen about heeling, you might occasionally offer a wonderful food treat or game so that your dog learns to associate the two activities (classical conditioning). If the wonderful thing is sufficiently wonderful, your dog should come to enjoy heeling.

On the other hand, you might use a combination of the two techniques. You might provide the dog with a taste of your wonderful treat or show him that you have his favorite toy with you, and then, when he offers you a particualrly wonderful response, you jackpot him. This would be a combination of *reinforcer sampling* and jackpotting. Reinforcer sampling is basically giving your dog a reason to respond well. We do this all the time. Mom shows you dessert (or maybe even gives you a small bite) and says this is what you'll get if you eat your veggies. I show Eejit that I have his special squeaky toy in my pocket and then I ask for a recall. The sample of the reinforcer serves to energize and motivate the dog.

I propose that we distinguish between jackpots (rewards for excellence) and *jumpstarts* (rewards to motivate). The combination of jumpstarting and jackpotting can be extremely effective. When I was training Shaahiin for Open, he had a very difficult time with the drop on recall. He would either slow down but refuse to drop or he would not come at all. He obviously found the drop extremely aversive in the context of the recall (his drops in other situations were just fine). I struggled with what to do and then on a whim, I brought my pet gerbil home from my office. I took the gerbil out to the training area, showed Shaahiin what I had in my pocket, and proceeded to set him up for the exercise. I called, he came charging in, I told him to down, and he dropped like a Border Collie. I released him and he came at top speed to nuzzle the gerbil (his reward - no, he didn't get to ingest it!). Well, the excellent response to the extremely powerful motivation was due to me allowing him to sample the reinforcer first - the jumpstart. But the fact that he never again had any problems with the drop on the drop-on-recall exercise I can only assume was due to the jackpot. It was as though he didn't understand how the two component responses (recall and drop) went together. Once he was motivated enough to try it without getting his knickers all in a knot, the lightbulb went on.

## The Recall Test

Here's something you can try with your dog to test the relative effectiveness of jackpots and jumpstarts. Mark two X's on the ground about 50' apart. Sit your dog on one X and stand at the other. Call your dog. Have a friend record, with a stop-watch, how many seconds it takes your dog to pass through a "finish line" marked about a foot before he reaches you. Reward him with a standard reinforcer. Repeat this until you begin to get consistent times. Then you can test the effectiveness of jackpotting by offering a special reward (maybe a whole liver muffin or something equally wonderful) for the next fastest recall. Do another 5-10 recalls with the standard reinforcer to see if your dog continues to maintain the speed of the recall you jackpotted. On another day, so the same thing but give the

dog a taste of your special reward first, before you leave him
(the jumpstart). Then see how fast he runs on that recall. Again,
does he maintain a faster speed even after you go back to the
usual reinforcer?

## Novelty

The novelty of a stimulus is important because in order for learning to occur, the animal must first notice the stimulus. Animals are
always more alert to novel stimuli. In classical conditioning, if a very
familiar stimulus is used as the CS, the animal will learn much more
slowly than if a novel stimulus is used. Particularly if the animal has
already been exposed to the stimulus and it has not been paired
with anything meaningful to the animal, it will be extremely difficult
to establish learning. This is called, in classical conditioning terms,
the CS-*preexposure effect*, and in operant conditioning terms, *learned
irrelevance*. Back in the section on single-event learning, I mentioned
that dogs probably come to class having learned the irrelevance of
commands like "come" and "stay". I tell owners if they have used
these commands frequently in the past to no avail, to change to a
different command when they begin actively teaching these responses.

## Timing

Timing is one factor that is critical for both classical and operant
conditioning, but for different reasons.

### Classical Conditioning

A load of research has been done to determine exactly the right
timing of the CS and the UCS, called the *interstimulus interval*. The
most important aspect seems to be the signaling power of the CS.

The CS has to occur *before* the UCS in order for learning to take place because the CS has to signal to the animal that the UCS is coming. If the UCS occurs before or even at the same time as the CS, then the animal doesn't need to pay attention to the CS and so doesn't learn the association.

That's why it is so tricky to condition a dog to eliminate on command. The unconditioned stimuli consist of both internal and external events that may be difficult for the trainer to pinpoint. The CS is a signal such as "Hurry up". If the command is delivered late, it may occur at the same time as the eliminative process starts (*simultaneous conditioning*) or it may even occur after the eliminative process

has already started (*backward conditioning*). Either way, the command does not serve to signal the start of the process and so the animal is unable to learn the association between the signal and the feelings that precede elimination. For effective learning, the CS must slightly

precede the UCS (*delay conditioning*). The command should be given during the stage when the dog is sniffing and circling, and continued until the dog begins eliminating - this ensures the signal is presented prior to and during the onset of elimination.

An easy way to understand this is to think about the signs on highways which warn of an impending curve in the road. The way this system is set up, you see the sign and have time to slow down before reaching the curve. This is analogous to delay conditioning (technically it is called trace conditioning because there is no overlap between the CS and the US). If you only saw the sign once you were in the middle of the curve, that would be simultaneous conditioning. Even worse, if the sign was posted after the curve, that would be like backward conditioning. Obviously, if the sign doesn't warn you in advance about the curve, it doesn't do you any good. Similarly, if the signal doesn't warn the dog in advance about the impending US, he won't learn about the CS-US association.

## Operant Conditioning

We all know that really good dog trainers have excellent timing. It is as though they are able to "read" the dog and recognize the signs that the dog is about to respond. This is ideal because the shorter the delay between the response and the reinforcer, the better for learning. A delay of even 1-2 seconds can be detrimental to learning. Think of it as the trainer conveying information to the dog about its behavior. If you time the information poorly, you are telling the dog something you don't intend. Say you tell your dog to sit and he does. However, you're distracted and don't acknowledge the response until 5 seconds later. During that 5 seconds, your dog could have looked at the ground, twiggled his ear, smelled an amazing crumb on the floor, and burped! Now which of these behaviors caused you to give him a cookie? How is he to know?

While you are reading this paper, you find $100 on the floor. Presumably, this functions as a reward for you. The $100 was left by an insane billionaire experimenter because, two hours ago at lunch, you ate gooseberry pie for desert instead of your usual apple pie.

The experimenter wanted to increase the future probability that you would eat gooseberry pie. It is very unlikely that this experiment will be successful… Hundreds of events are bound to occur during the two hours between consumption of the gooseberry pie and the receipt of the $100… The odds are very great that you would have associated one of these intervening events with the $100 and that this would have drowned out the association with the still earlier gooseberry pie. (Revusky & Garcia, 1970, p 20)

**Primary and Secondary Reinforcers**. Fortunately, there is a way around the problem of having to deliver reinforcement immediately. It isn't always very easy to stuff a piece of food in your dog's mouth the instant he does something you like. Up to now, whenever I mention reinforcement, I have assumed that the reward is a *primary* or *unconditioned* reinforcer. A primary reinforcer is something the dog intrinsically likes, such as food, water, play, cuddling from mom, going for a walk in the park, etc. There are also *secondary* or *conditioned* reinforcers; these are things that initially the dog has no interest in but because of their association with a primary reinforcer, come to be important to him. An example is the dog's name. At first, my puppy had no idea that the word "Eejit" had any significance for him. It didn't take long, however, for him to learn that "Eejit" preceded all kinds of neat things: dinner, walks, play, etc. *Precede* is the operative word here - in order for a stimulus to become a conditioned rein- forcer, it must always precede the primary reinforcer. It has to *signal* to the dog that the primary reinforcer is likely to follow (via classical conditioning). The neat thing is that a conditioned reinforcer can be a sound, which is much easier to deliver immediately when the behavior occurs (easier than primary reinforcers).

The first thing a rat or a pigeon learns when placed in a Skinner box is the sound of the feeder operating. The feeder always makes a sound just befor ethe food drops into the cup. This is called *magazine training* and the purpose of this is to establish the feeder sound as a conditioned reinforcer. Then when the rat begins to sniff around the lever or the pigeon wanders over in the direction of the pecking key, the feeder sound can be used to reinforce the behavior. Without this prior conditioning, the experimenter would have to wait until the animal noticed the food in the feeder and then whatever behavior immediately preceded the discovery (probably sniffing the air or the ground) would be reinforced.

Most dog owners use "Good Dog" to convey to the dog when they like what he is doing. These words become a conditioned reinforcer for the dog. We manage to say "Good Dog" as we struggle to get a cookie out of a pocket to reward a nice sit in the park and this conditioned reinforcer serves to "bridge" the time between the dog's response and the reinforcer. The dog is being provided the informa-tion regarding what aspect of its behavior earned the treat, even though we aren't able to present the treat at exactly the correct moment. The conditioned reinforcer also comes to have value itself and so the primary reinforcer need not always follow.

More and more trainers are now using what is called a "cricket" or "clicker" as a conditioned reinforcer. The clicker is often an easier tool to use as a conditioned reinforcer than a "Good Dog" phrase. This is because trainers are more careful with the clicker than they are with words and so the clicker is "protected" from losing its value as a conditioned reinforcer (it doesn't get used

noncontingently). Furthermore, the sound of the click is more obvi-ous to the trainer than her own voice and consequently, delays between the response and the click are more obvious to the trainer.

The distinctive sound a clicker makes travels distance well and so you are able to reinforce behavior that occurs at a distance from you. Anything that improves the ability of the trainer to convey information to the dog will improve the dog's ability to learn.

One limitation of the clicker is that it is of a fixed, very short duration. We know that the most effective CS is one that overlaps in time with the US. More and more marine mammal trainers are using whistles because you can control how long the whistle sounds. The idea is to blow the whistle until the food is available (at least when you are establishing the association between the two). That way there is a definite overlap between the sound and the food. Because dog trainers use their voices a lot, whistles are not ideal. Some trainers use a distinctive, unique sound they can make with their voice, such as "Psst". Ideally someone will come up with a noise like a buzzer that we can sound for a second or two. Classical conditioning is maximal when the signal is still on when the primary reinforcer is delivered.

It may help you to think of conditioning your cliker as if you are charging a battery. When you buy a battery, you don't immediately begin using it. You have to charge it first. Likewise, make sure you charge your conditioned reinforcer before you begin using it. Each time you pair the sound with the treat, you up the charge a bit. You need to charge the sound well before using it to reward a behavior. Then, each time you use the sound to reward a behavior, without also delivering a treat (when you are on an intermittent schedule), the charge drops a bit. You must charge your conditioned reinforcer well to begin with and then ensure it maintains it strength by recharging at frequent intervals. Each time you click and treat, you charge. Each time you click with no treat, you lose a bit of charge.

One issue that comes up in discussions of conditioned reinforcers is whether you can use a conditioned reinforcer to reward an ongoing behavior without the dog stopping to return to you for his anticipated treat. This is something the dog would have to learn - when he hears the sound, there would have to be an additional signal which tells him whether to continue or to cease responding. If you are using the conditioned reinforcer in a situation where the dog has already learned a sequence of responses, such as retrieving a dumbell, the dog may be able to figure out for himself to continue the behavior when he hears the sound. Some trainers use two different signals - one which "marks" behaviors but is not specifically associated with reward (it would have to be established as a conditioned reinforcer initially to have any lasting meaning to the dog) and one which serves to signal imminent reinforcement. Ramba recommends using two different words "good" and "out". "Good" is initially established as a conditioned reinforcer but then later is used in situations where the dog is expected to continue working. "Out" always signals the end of a sequence of behaviors and a primary reinforcer.

You'll often hear trainers say that the conditioned reinforcer "marks" the correct behavior or the feature of the behavior that you like. It's like your dog could take a flash photo of the behavior he has just emitted. It is definitely true that a conditioned reinforcer serves this function. What is less obvious is that any stimulus, any event that is noticed by the animal, will also serve the same purpose. You can "mark" a behavior with a stimulus your dog has never, ever encountered before and it will influence how easily he learns what behavior you intermittently reinforce with a primary reinforcer. Really, though, this would only be important to know if you find yourself on a deserted island with no clicker or whistle and you also have laryngitis! When your dog performs a behavior you like, mark it with anything - jump up and down, throw sand around, do anything! You won't have missed a valuable teaching opportunity!

### Establishing a Conditioned Reinforcer

An easy way to teach the significance of the clicker is to sit around and watch TV, with a container of treats and the clicker in hand. Keep the clicker in one hand and a treat in the other hand, which should be closed around the treat. Sound the clicker and open your hand to allow the dog to take the treat. Say nothing. If the dog doesn't clue in to take the treat from your hand, toss the treat on the floor to start. Continue to do this click → treat pairing numerous times but be sure to vary the time between pairings. Sometimes wait 30 s, sometimes wait a minute, sometimes wait just a few seconds before repeating the click → treat pairing. Be sure to sound the clicker suddenly, without any preparatory movements, such as reaching for the food. Get the next piece of food in your hand immediately after the dog has taken one so this does not become a cue for the dog that you are about to click again. The sound of the clicker must be the only cue the dog has as to the availability of the food in the hand. If for some reason, the dog does not take the food within a second or two, close your hand up again and save that piece for the next time. You don't want the dog to eat the food without hearing the click just before. Most dogs will go to incredible efforts to solicit the food from you - he might watch you intently, jump on you, nuzzle the hand that holds the treat or the clicker, and so on. You should ignore these behaviors and carry on. You should not always wait for the dog to stop before sounding the clicker because you will be inadvertently teaching the dog that the way to get the clicker to sound is to sit or lie quietly and do nothing. This may be counter to what you may want to teach later. I like to have my computer pro- duce a schedule for me to follow - set a timer for each interval and sound the clicker regardless of what the dog is doing. This way I can be sure I'm not consistently associating the click with any specific behavior. I also get into the notion of thinking of myself as an artifi- cial feeder, simply opening and closing the hand as determined by the schedule. Then I can resist the urge to talk to the dog, to re- spond to his solicitations, and possibly then convey the impending click in some way. You want to continue this "magazine training" until the dog will jump up or come running when he hears the click.

Test this by waiting until the dog is distracted by something, then sound the clicker. If he turns to you immediately and takes the food, he has learned the significance of the click signal and you are ready to use the clicker as a conditioned reinforcer.

(Adapted from Skinner, 1951).

## Schedules of Reinforcement

A schedule of reinforcement is a program or rule that determines how and when a response will be followed by a reward. When the dog responds, should he always be given a treat or a click? This should depend upon the stage of learning. Specifically, it should depend upon whether the dog has learned the relationship between the response and the consequence or not. This is important because the reinforcement schedule influences both how the response is learned and how the response is maintained. The schedule should not be the same for both.

### The Different Types of Schedules

1 Under a continuous reinforcement schedule, every occurrence of the response is followed by reinforcement. The abbreviation is CRF.

2 Under a partial or intermittent reinforcement schedule (PRF), responding is reinforced only after certain responses. The schedules are fixed ratio (FR), variable ratio (VR), random ratio (RR), fixed interval (FI), variable interval (VI).

3 Under a differential reinforcement schedule, only certain rates of responding or certain types of responses are reinforced.

a. With differential *rate* schedules, whether or not a response is rewarded depends on how soon the response occurred after the preceding response. The schedules are differential reinforcement of high rates of behavior (DRH) and differential reinforcement of low rates of behavior (DRL).

b. With differential *type* schedules, whether or not a response is rewarded depends on the form (or quality) of the response. The schedules are differential reinforcement of other behavior (DRO), differential reinforcement of incompatible behavior (DRI), and differential reinforcement of excellent behavior (DRE).

4 Under a duration reinforcement schedule, responding must be maintained throughout an entire interval for reinforcement to be earned. The schedules are fixed duration (FD), variable duration (VD), and random duration (RD).

**Discrete-Trials Experiments.** When researchers first looked at schedules of reinforcement, they were studying rats running down alleys to get food in a goal box. This is called a *discrete-trials* proce- dure because the rat can only run down the alley if he is placed in the apparatus by the experimenter. Each opportunity to run the alley is considered a separate (discrete) trial. Training a dog is often based on discrete trials: you request a response and the dog is rewarded for responding correctly. The dog doesn't respond on his own. If he does, he is not rewarded. For instance, your dog sits a lot but you only reward those that occur as a result of your request.

What the rat-runners discovered was that if the rats were ran- domly rewarded only 50% of the time (called a *random ratio* or RR schedule), they actually ran faster (particularly as they got closer to the goal box) than when rewarded every time. They explained this by saying that the rat comes to expect his reward and if he doesn't get it, he becomes frustrated and this frustration actually serves as motivation for him to run faster as he approaches the goal box.

Bear in mind that this change in speed is dependent upon the randomness of reward delivery. If the rewards are delivered system- atically, the changes in speed are also systematic. For instance, if a rat is trained on a regular schedule with rewarded trials (R) and nonrewarded (N) trials occurring in strict alternation (RNRNRNRN), at first he runs faster on N trials than on R trials because on N trials he just had a reward on the previous trial and so that reward serves to motivate him to run faster the next chance. On R trials he just experienced no reward and so he is less keen to get down the alley fast. However, after extensive experience with this schedule, the rat learns to run faster on R trials than on N trials; he has learned that the two outcomes alternate and so if he isn't rewarded one time, then he knows he will be the next time.

Another researcher wanted to see if rats could learn more complex schedules such as RRNNRRNN and RNNRNNRNN. As long as the rats could tell from the previous trials what would happen the next time, they would learn whether to expect a reward or not, even with delays of up to 30 minutes between trials (so they had to remember what happened on the last trial). I guess if the lowly rat can accomplish this, then any dog who has ever been in a ring more than once in his life should learn pretty quickly that an obedience trial situation and a nervous handler signal an N trial!

The lesson in this is that as a trainer, you need to vary the rewards randomly so the dog cannot possibly anticipate whether he will be rewarded or not. Don't reach into your pocket on R trials and not on N trials. Don't give two rewards and then skip one, two more and then skip one - he'll figure you out. Being random is a challenge, though. Psychologists have looked at how good people are at behaving randomly and guess what? We aren't, we're notoriously systematic. I often ask my computer to generate a random series of Rs and Ns and I mark them off as I go through to guard against my own inadequate randomness.

**Free-Operant Experiments.** If you've read much about operant conditioning at all, you've probably come across such terms as interval and ratios schedules. These types of schedules are used in *free-operant* procedures. In a free-operant procedure, the animal is free to respond whenever he chooses. For instance, a rat in a Skinner

box has a bar that is always available and the rat goes up and
presses it for food whenever he wants. Reinforcement schedules
have been studied extensively in free-operant situations and the
effects are revealed in how often the animal responds. The frequency
of responding doesn't translate directly to discrete trials because the
animal can't vary how frequently it responds. Your dog might retrieve
his dumbbell constantly if given the opportunity but you only throw
it when you want him to retrieve it. During heeling, there are a
number of behaviors that occur as they are requested: the sit, the
change in speed, the turns, the halts. However, the dog should also
be rewarded for eye contact and this the dog is expected to do,
umprompted. The frequency of eye contact is an example of a free
operant behavior. See the distinction?

## Ratio Schedules

1 On a *continuous reinforcement schedule* (CRF), every response is followed by a reward. This is the best schedule to use when first
teaching a new behavior. An animal on a CRF schedule responds
at a steady, moderate rate with brief and unpredictable pauses.
Responding gradually slows as the animal becomes satiated with
the reinforcer.

2 On a *fixed ratio schedule of reinforcement* (FR), there is a fixed ratio
between the number of responses made and the number of
rewards earned[5]. On an FR-5 schedule, the animal must make five
responses before earning a reward. If it makes ten responses, it
will get two rewards. The number following the FR refers to the
number of responses required for each reward. Essentially, the
more the animal does, the more rewards it will earn. For humans,
this is known as piecework or performance-contingent pay. An
animal or human on a FR schedule responds at a high, very steady
rate except immediately following reinforcement. This is called

[5] A CRF schedule is also known as a FR-1 schedule.

the *post-reinforcement pause*. It is as though the animal is mustering strength for a long bout of work before another reward (the Monday morning blahs). The more responses the animal has to make for each reward, the longer the pause.

**3** On a *variable ratio schedule of reinforcement* (VR), the number of responses required for each reinforcer varies from one occasion to the next. The number following the VR refers to the number of responses required, *on average*, for each reward. For instance, a VR-5 schedule means that, on average, the animal must respond five times before being reinforced but it might require as many as ten this time and only two the next and so on. On a VR schedule, the animal responds at a high, steady rate with a minimal post-reinforcement pause (because this time it might only have to do one or two to get the goodie and these experiences carry more weight in the animal's memory). Slot machines are often designed on VR schedules. Sales people who work on commission are usually on VR schedules. There is some chance of success with every response that is made and the more you respond, the more often you will be rewarded.

Intermittent Schedule of Reward.

If the requirement on a ratio schedule is too high, the animal will take breaks or stop working altogether. This means that the animal is not prepared to put in that much effort for the amount of reinforcement received. Theoretically, if it takes more energy to get the goodie than the goodie provides, the animal should be unwilling to do it. We know that's not strictly true because some dogs will go to tremendous lengths for a tiny taste of Rollover but they will stop working if the demand is raised too quickly. This is called *ratio strain*. A pigeon will happily peck on a FR-200 schedule if the ratio is raised slowly but if it is raised too quickly, say straight from FR-20 to FR-200, the bird will likely stop responding altogether.

### Interval Schedules

**1** On a *fixed interval schedule of reinforcement* (FI), a reward is delivered only if a response occurs after a specified period of time has elapsed. For instance, on a FI-5 second schedule, the animal is rewarded for the first response that occurs *after* five seconds has elapsed since the last reward. If the animal responds after two seconds, nothing happens. If the animal responds after six seconds, the response is rewarded. Notice that it is not sufficient to just wait for the time to elapse. There still has to be a response before a reward will be delivered. If you are anxious for your mail delivery and it reliably comes at 11:15 am, there is no point in visiting the mailbox any earlier. However, your mail might be there at 11:20 but it won't do you any good if you don't make the response of visiting the mailbox. You have to wait and then you have to make the response in order to be rewarded. Because responses made immediately after the delivery of food never result in reinforcement (i.e., there is no point in checking the mailbox again in the afternoon if you've already received that day's mail), the animal learns to wait and be patient between responses. Few responses occur right after a reward but as the interval times down, more and more responses occur (if you weren't able to tell time, you might start visiting the mailbox mid-morning of the next day). The layoff right after a reward is called a *fixed-interval scallop* (it is similar to the post-reinforcement pause).

**2** On a *variable interval schedule of reinforcement* (VI), the interval that is required to elapse before a reward can be earned varies. For instance, on a VI-5 second schedule, a response will only be reinforced if it occurs at least five seconds, on average, since the last reinforcement. But on each specific occasion, the animal might only have to wait one or two seconds or as long as nine or ten seconds before a response earns a reward. Like VR schedules, VI schedules lead to steady response rates without pauses. The overall rate of responding is a function of the time interval (shorter intervals will produce higher response rates). Imagine that you are anxiously trying to contact someone by telephone and their line is frequently busy. If you ring again too soon, you may not be rewarded because the line will still be busy. But if you wait a long time before ringing again, you may have waited too long and really, you could have spoken to the person sooner. The delivery of electronic mail is on a VI schedule. If you are eagerly anticipating a response to a posting, you might check frequently. Most of the time, say ,there is nothing but every now and then, you receive a useful response. How frequently that happens will determine how often you check

In standard interval schedules, once the reward becomes available, the animal can obtain it whenever he chooses to respond. For instance, the interval is 30 seconds but the animal might not respond until two or three minutes later. The first response will still be rewarded. Interval schedules can be complicated with the introduction of a *limited hold*. A limited hold means that the reward is only available for a certain length of time after the interval has elapsed. If the animal doesn't respond within that time frame, the reward is lost. This is the usual setup in university residence cafeterias. The meal is available at a certain time and the student need only turn up at the cafeteria to obtain the food. But the meal is not available indefinitely. If the student waits too long before turning up, everything will have been cleared and put away and food will not be available again until the next scheduled mealtime.

Those of you who are parents may be familiar with *The Timer Game*, which is an example of a VI schedule with a limited hold of 0 seconds. The Timer Game can be played in any situation where you have children confined to a small space with limited activities, such as a long car trip or an airplane or train ride. It goes like this: you set the timer for an amount of time but the children can't see it time down. When it rings, the behavior of each child is assessed. If the child is behaving appropriately, a primary or conditioned reinforcer is dispensed (for instance, you could have them earn tokens to trade for TV viewing time later that evening). If the child is not behaving appropriately, no reinforcement is earned or may even be taken away (i.e., TV time is subtracted from the child's total). The reinforcement schedule is a VI because it is based entirely on time and the interval of time is unknown to the child (technically, it is a *random interval* schedule because there is no mean time around which the intervals vary). The limited hold is 0 seconds because the child must be emitting the desired response exactly when the interval times down. Theoretically, the child could scream, yell, and throw temper tantrums throughout the interval but provided she was behaving at the precise moment the timer dings, she would legitimately earn reinforcement. That's the essence of an interval schedule.

The diagram (on the next page) displays the different patterns of responding on different schedules. The lines show cumulative responses; in other words, the line increases a bit with each response made by the animal. The hash marks indicate when a reinforcement is delivered. The VR schedule shows the highest rate of responding, with the VI schedule a close second. Remember, though, this is free-operant responding, where animals can control the rate at which they respond. In a discrete-trials situation, such as most dog training exercises, reinforcement schedules affect the speed or intensity of the response, not the rate of responding.

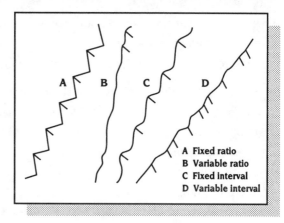

A Fixed ratio
B Variable ratio
C Fixed interval
D Variable interval

## Differential Reinforcement Schedules

Differential reinforcement schedules are quite distinct and have been used primarily in applied settings with both humans and animals.

1 *Response rate schedules* require that the animal respond at a certain rate in order to obtain reinforcement. Whether any specific response earns a reward depends on how soon it has occurred after the preceding response. For instance, you could set up a schedule in which a response is reinforced only if it occurs *within* five seconds of the preceding response. If the animal responds after six seconds has elapsed, no reward would be delivered and the animal would need to respond again within five seconds in order to earn a reward. This is called a *differential reinforcement of high rates* (DRH) schedule and it encourages animals to respond at a high rate. Conversely, an animal could be on a schedule in which a specific response would earn a reward only if it occurred *after* a certain time had elapsed since the previous response. This is called a *differential reinforcement of low rates* (DRL) schedule and it encourages animals to respond slowly. Workers on assembly lines often face a conflict between these two schedules: the faster they work, the better management likes it (DRH) but the slower they

work, the better their fellow employees like it (DRL) because no one is pushing the standard too high. Rate schedules are not really very useful for most dog training situations.

**2** *Response type schedules* require that the response be of a certain form or quality before earning reinforcement. These types of schedules are often used to encourage appropriate behaviors while at the same time, eliminating inappropriate behaviors. For instance, if your dog likes to jump up, you could place him on a schedule in which only responses that cannot be done at the same time as jumping up would be rewarded. This is called *differential reinforcement of incompatible behaviors* (DRI) or *alternative response training* or *countercommanding*. By rewarding only incompatible behaviors, you strengthen the tendency for these behaviors to be repeated and

so the jumping up will become less likely because the dog can't do both. Alternatively, you might simply reward any behavior other than jumping up, whether it be incompatible or not. This is called *differential reinforcement of other behaviors* (DRO) and it works on the same principle. If you're being rewarded for doing something else, you probably won't bother doing what is considered objectionable. The final schedule, called *differential reinforcement of excellent behaviors* (DRE), can't be found in any psychology textbook. But it is the type of schedule that is most appropriate for the majority of responses we train dogs to perform. Most responses can vary in quality: a sit could be faster, a front could be straighter. Rather than reward such responses randomly, it makes more sense to reward these responses differentially and reward those that come closest to perfection. This is in contrast to the all-or-none type responses that animals in the lab perform. A rat pressing a bar or a pigeon pecking a key just has to press or peck hard enough to operate a switch. The response is either sufficient or it isn't. This is more like a dog operating a flyball box - the ball is either released or it isn't.

This is sort of like jackpot rewards for excellence, except that I'm suggesting you work toward excellence with all your reinforcements. Of course, what you consider to be excellent will depend upon the dog's stage of learning. When acquiring a new behavior, all responses are excellent. As your dog learns, most behaviors will be better than a few and those should be reinforced. As your dog refines his behavior, so you adapt your criterion for excellence. When he reaches the stage of maintenance, you may be selectively reinforcing only the most amazing responses.

## Duration Schedules

Duration schedules are included in this section but technically these are not schedules of reinforcement. Duration schedules require that the animal maintain a particular level of responding throughout an entire interval of time in order to earn reinforcement. A classic example is the stay exercise in obedience training. The dog must maintain a specific position for a period of time. Although in competition, the times are set (a fixed duration schedule), in training, the dog is more accustomed to times that vary (either systematically, as with a variable duration schedule, or not so systematically, as with a random duration schedule). Obviously, in addition to teaching the dog to perform the desired response, the trainer then has to teach the dog to maintain the response over time. This is also known as threshold training. At first, the dog is required to stay for only a very short time (i.e., 1-2 seconds) but gradually, that time is increased to the more realistic goal of several minutes. The reason why duration schedules are not really reinforcement schedules is that the animal is really being trained to perform a quantitatively different response: one that takes longer and longer. The reinforcement usually follows the end of the time period, although in training, it may come at any time during the interval as well. For instance, the trainer working on the out-of-sight stay should return at random times to reinforce the dog for maintaining the sit response. As the dog becomes more comfortable with the exercise, the trainer should decrease the number of returns, with occasional surprises thrown in to keep the dog attentive.

For dogs that have difficulty with stays, the key is to gradually increase the time requirement. If the dog can maintain a sit-stay for 20 seconds on average, the trainer should reinforce the behavior at approximately 10 seconds, say, but then ensure that the response continues through the reinforcement (the dog must continue sitting even though it is being reinforced and then continue to maintain the sit response after reinforcement). Once the dog is demonstrating the ability to maintain the sit for a full 20 seconds, with one reinforcement around 10 seconds and one at the end, the trainer should delay the first reinforcement until 12-13 seconds. This should mean that the dog can maintain the full sit-stay for 22-23 seconds before the final reinforcement. Continue to work on delaying the first reinforcement delivery and, at the same time, you should be able to delay the final reinforcement as well. At some point, you may want to include additional reinforcement deliveries as the full amount of time increases. By approaching threshold training systematically, it is surprising how quickly an animal can learn to maintain a behavior for long periods of time. This approach is also very applicable to treating dogs with separation anxiety (see later section on problem behaviors).

## Which Reinforcement Schedule Should You Use?

When teaching a new behavior, it is most efficient to use a CRF schedule so that every response is rewarded. Once your dog has displayed that he has learned the association between the response and the reward, you should gradually shift to an intermittent schedule.

How do you know when your dog has learned a response? I have heard people throw out numbers, such as continuously reinforce 75-150 consecutive responses before moving to an intermittent schedule. The truth of the matter is that the optimum is going to depend upon the behavior and the dog. Easy responses are acquired more quickly than difficult ones. Some dogs will catch on to certain behaviors more quickly than others. When instructing pet owners, I also err on the side of caution. I'd much rather they overtrain something than undertrain it. However, maintaining a behavior on a CRF schedule for a long period makes it harder to move to an intermittent schedule. For experienced trainers, you should always be pushing your dog. If he begins to fall apart, back up. It is far better to challenge your dog and keep him interested than it is to bore him with stuff that's too easy and predictable. If you have moved too fast, he'll let you know. It's kind of like children in school. If the bright kids are held back with the slower kids, they become bored and restless. If they are constantly being challenged by their teachers, they continue to progress at a rapid pace. Your dog is likely going to be bright about some things and slow about others. Take risks but be flexible!

How do you know what intermittent schedule to use? For all-or-none responses, a random ratio (RR) or variable ratio (VR) schedule is appropriate. For more complex responses that can vary in quality, a differential schedule which rewards only the best responses (DRE) seems most appropriate. For eliminating certain problem behaviors, a differential schedule such as DRL, DRO, and DRI might be a consideration.

How many responses you should require for each reward depends upon the nature of the response. I have heard all sorts of numbers suggested, anything from 1 reinforcement for every 2 responses to 1 reinforcement for as many as 20 responses. In fact, individual dogs vary in how much they will work for a reinforcement and of course, the nature of the reinforcement is important as well. A Border Collie might well sit 30 times for the opportunity to chase a Frisbee while a Saluki would be bored out of his mind long before you managed 30 sits for virtually any reinforcer! For rats running down an alleyway, which is a simple, though time-consuming behavior, they need to find food in the goal box 50-75% of the time to maintain a good running speed. If you drop them drown to 25%, they begin to run very slowly.

Generally speaking, if it is a relatively simple response, such as a sit, you can use a fairly demanding schedule. My dogs are often required to sit at least a dozen times on a walk for no reinforcement. If it is a complex response, such as a retrieve, a richer schedule that provides frequent rewards is probably necessary to maintain the behavior. Unfortunately, there is no easy answer to the question of the optimum intermittent schedule. It very much depends upon the animal, the response, and the reinforcement.

Randomness is the critical issue. I see many dogs that appear to have learned that during heeling, their handler never rewards while on the move (presumably because it is more difficult to deliver a reward while moving). The dog's attention shifts from the handler until the handler slows to a halt. Suddenly the dog is attentive to the handler because he has learned that the handler only rewards him on the halts. Ah, you say, you could deliver conditioned reinforcement during the moving parts of the exercise and primary reinforcement during the stationary parts. Well, you could bu tyour dog would quickly figure out that as well.

Even more challenging is the dog that has learned not to expect a reward if he has just received one (an interval scallop). These dogs will shift their attention away from the handler for brief periods of time immediately after being given a reward. Adept handlers ensure occasional rewards are given in quick succession to avoid this problem, while other handlers avoid the problem by simply breaking off the exercise after each primary reward.

Remember that although conditioned reinforcers do function similarly to primary reinforcers, they cannot sustain as demanding a schedule as can primary reinforcers. What I mean is that if you can get, on average, 10 sits from your dog for one primary reinforcer, you cannot also expect to get 10 sits for one conditioned reinforcer. You might, however, be able to get 20 sits with one primary and four conditioned reinforcers.

Technically, a partial reinforcement schedule implies that some responses receive no reward whatsoever, be it a primary or a conditioned reinforcer. However, in reality, we usually do choose to provide some feedback to the animal, particularly if the animal is also in a position to emit other incorrect behaviors (for instance, the dog that is not yet under good stimulus control and offers a whole sequence of behaviors in response to one command). The main concern should be that the animal can discriminate the difference between incorrect responses and responses that are correct but not reinforced. Many laboratory experiments do provide conditioned reinforcement on a CRF schedule (say, for instance, the feeder clicks but no food is dropped), while the primary reinforcement is delivered intermittently for correct responses. Others incorporate a procedure in which correct but unrewarded responses have no consequence, while incorrect responses lead to a brief time-out (the box might go dark for a few seconds).

Gary Wilkes's "Wrong" or Jean Donaldson's "Too bad" function in this manner. Because "Wrong" signals "no reward" it becomes a conditioned aversive stimulus. Correct responses are followed either by reinforcement or no response from the trainer. The lack of any response from the trainer can become a conditioned reinforcer, which signals that the preceding response was correct but unreinforced. Anything that serves to differentiate incorrect responses from correct but unreinforced responses will make learning more efficient. I recommend incorporating both a conditioned aversive stimulus (one that has signaled no reward, **not** one that has signaled a punishment) for incorrect responses, a conditioned reinforcer for correct but unreinforced responses, and both a primary reinforcer and the conditioned reinforcer for correct, reinforced responses.

## What About Reinforcement Schedules in Classical Conditioning?

During acquisition, the learning of both classically conditioned responses and operant responses is best with continuous reinforcement. However, although partial reinforcement of an operant response tends to make the response even stronger, quite the opposite is true with classical conditioning. Learning is best maintained when the UCS <u>always</u> follows the CS. If the UCS follows the CS intermittently, it might take longer to get a CR, the response might be weaker than the UCR, or you may not even get the CR consistently. The most efficient classical conditioning procedure involves a consistent relationship between the CS and the UCS. The one major exception to this is the conditioned emotional response (see later section). Such responses can be classically conditioned with only sporadic pairings of the CS and the UCS.

## Premack's Theory of Reinforcement

David Premack, back in the mid-1960s, developed an idea about reinforcement that was very different from most views. He proposed that the opportunity to engage in particular types of activities could serve as reinforcers. Operant responses, such as sitting, and responses associated with reinforcement, such as eating, differ only in how frequently they are likely to occur. Dogs that are deprived of food are highly likely to engage in eating behaviors whenever possible. By contrast, sitting is not going to occur with any great frequency. If, however, eating is made contingent upon sitting, then sitting will also occur with high likelihood.

This idea is not new. Another term for Premack's Theory is "Gramma's Law" which is "eat your veggies and you can have dessert". A good thing can reinforce engaging in a not-so-good thing. Premack demonstrated the effectiveness of his theory by giving young children two alternative activities. They could either play pinball or they could eat candy. He found that some of the children preferred eating candy to playing pinball and some preferred playing pinball to eating candy. He then put half the children in a condition where eating candy was the reinforcer and playing pinball was the operant response. In other words, every time the child played pinball, he was given the opportunity to eat candy. If a child wanted to eat candy, she had to play pinball first. What Premack found was that only those children who preferred eating candy to playing pinball increased their rate of playing pinball (over and above the children who preferred pinball anyway). The other group of children experienced the opposite: every time they ate candy, they were given the opportunity to play pinball. If a child wanted to play pinball, she had to eat candy first. And only those children who preferred playing pinball to eating candy increased the frequency of eating candy

The animal's motivational state makes a huge difference as to whether an activity will be reinforcing or not. A dog that is deprived of water will work very hard to obtain water. A dog that is deprived of exercise will do all sorts of things to gain the opportunity to exercise. In fact, a thirsty dog can be made to exercise extensively in order to earn access to water, while a bored, restless dog will drink buckets of water in order to earn access to a field for running.

As a puppy, Eejit provided me with a nice example of Premack's theory. At the beginning of a run in the park, Eejit was highly moti-

Experiment 1.

1 Dog is water deprived     2 Dog drinks more than he runs.     3. Time — Drinking reinforces running

Experiment 2.

1 Dog is not water deprived     2 Dog runs more than he drinks.     3. Time — Running reinforces drinking

vated to chase and retrieve the Frisbee. He rarely solicited me to kick snow or leaves for him. After 10-20 minutes, though, he was much more likely to engage in soliciting behavior for kicking than he was to chase the Frisbee. I used this to my advantage because I wanted to teach him to retrieve the Frisbee directly to my hand. Rather than reward him with food, which would alter his motivational state from one of play to one of food-soliciting, I decided to reward retrieving to hand with our kicking game. Whenever he returned the Frisbee to my hand voluntarily, I immediately began kicking snow for him. If he returned with the Frisbee but dropped it at the ground near my feet (the more likely scenario), I would request that he pick it up. If he did, I started kicking snow. If he did not, Ciaran would pick up the Frisbee and I would throw it for him (also a game that Eejit enjoys because he can herd Ciaran). Very quickly, Eejit figured out that if he engaged in a low probability behavior (returning the Frisbee to my hand), he could earn the opportunity to engage in a high probability behavior (jumping for kicked snow).

Premack's theory has been useful in applied settings with children as well. Children with autism often engage in repetitive aberrant behaviors, such as waving hands, making noises, rubbing objects, etc. In one experiment, children were required to engage in scholarly activities (naming objects, responding to questions, counting coins, etc.) either for a preferred candy as the reward or for the opportunity to engage in an aberrant behavior for 3-5 seconds (something which they are normally discouraged from doing). In all cases, the chance to engage in the aberrant behavior resulted in better performance on the tasks than the food reinforcement.

This is why it works so well for dog trainers to allow their dogs to jump up on them as a reinforcer. Presumably the dogs are not normally permitted to jump up and so this is a highly preferred behavior with a low probability of occurrence. Ian Dunbar uses Premack's Theory in his writings. He recommends using "life rewards" to reinforce good behavior. Life rewards are high probability behaviors. If the dog sits, he gets his dinner. If he stays while the door is being opened, he gets to go for a walk.

I once tried working Ciaran's weave poles (in this scenario, the lower probability behavior) next to a pen of Indian runner ducks (herding is his ultimate high probability behavior!). If he moved through the poles correctly and at a good speed, he was permitted to run to the pen and herd the ducks for a period of time. If he made an error, he had to repeat the poles again. Boy, did he learn to weave quickly and accurately!

The biggest drawback with Premack's approach to reinforcement is that, often, life rewards are impractical. It's fine to reinforce a good recall with the opportunity to chase a squirrel but then you have to go through great contortions to get your dog back again to conduct another training trial. Life rewards usually take time to complete and often shift the dog's focus away from you entirely and you end up working to get the dog refocused back on work. Another interesting research finding is that, at least for people, the chance to engage in the rewarding behavior sometimes isn't considered as "good" when you have to earn it. In one study, a woman had to spend a certain amount of time studying (a low probability behavior) in order to earn time to knit (a high probability behavior). She reported that she began to feel resentful about the setup and didn't enjoy her knitting time as much as she normally did. Studies with animals suggest a similar effect: they don't always end up working for the life rewards as much as you would expect. Sometimes, they simply change preferences as well. It has been several months since I faded out the contingency for Eejit regarding the Frisbee. Now he seems to enjoy retrieving the Frisbee just as much as he enjoys me kicking for him.

# Stimulus (Signal) Control

Stimulus control is a fundamental component of animal training because this is the process that allows us to put behaviors on cue. If a behavior reliably happens in response to a specific cue or cues and not to others, the behavior is under stimulus or signal control. With classically conditioned responses, the stimuli that control responding are called conditioned stimuli (the CSs). With operant conditioning, the stimuli that control responding are called discriminative stimuli ($S^D$s). Understanding what animals learn about stimuli will help you to make training as clear as possible to your dog.

This is another area where classical and operant conditioning gets muddied up. As you already know, in classical conditioning, the initially neutral stimulus known as the CS comes to elicit a conditioned response as a result of its association with the UCS. The conditioned response comes under the control of the CS. In operant conditioning, the discriminative stimulus signals to the animal when to perform the response:

$$S^D \rightarrow R \rightarrow S^{R+}$$

The popular notion is that operant conditioning really consists of a classical association between the $S^D$ and the response-reinforcer contingency. In other words, the $S^D$ comes to signal to the animal when a response will result in reinforcement. Just because your dog's sitting behavior is under stimulus control, so that when you say "sit", he does, that doesn't mean that every time he sits, he does so because of the possibility of a reward. Sometimes he just wants to sit. The $S^D$, your command "sit", signals to the dog that now there is a consequence for sitting and he decides if it would be in his best interest to do so.

Behavior always occurs in the presence of particular stimuli and whether you intend it or not, these stimuli will affect your dog's learning. If you are teaching an operant response, your dog he has two problems to figure out:

- he has to learn which of his behaviors produces the reward (i.e. that sitting results in a cookie).

- he has to learn which stimuli or environmental cues <u>predict</u> when that behavior will produce the reward (i.e. that the word "sit" tells him when the behavior of sitting will result in a cookie).

In other words, the dog learns that the sit → cookie relationship is operative only when it is preceded by the word "sit". In the absence of the word "sit", sitting produces nothing.

Animals learn the first problem first - they learn *what* behavior to do. They learn *when* to do it second. Think about it. What happens when your dog learns to roll over? He does it all the time. He does it no matter what you say. You pick up the treat bag and there he is - rolling over. He has learned that rolling over produces good things but he hasn't yet figured out the S$^D$ that tells him when rolling over produces a good thing.

## Discrimination and Generalization

Stimulus control involves two contradictory processes. On the one hand, the animal has to learn to *discriminate* the relevant stimuli from all the other stimuli that are present when the response is reinforced. The dog has to learn that the words "roll over" predict that the response of rolling over will be reinforced. The dog also has to learn that other features of the situation, such as which TV program was on, the shoes you were wearing, and so on and so forth are not predictors of anything to do with rolling over. The dog also has to learn that other commands, such as "fetch it" do not predict that rolling over will be reinforced. Discriminating means that the response will be offered in the presence of the S$^D$ and not in the presence of other stimuli.

On the other hand, the dog has to learn to *generalize* across similar stimuli. The dog has to learn that the phrase "roll over" means that the response of rolling over will be reinforced whether you whisper it or shout it, whether you ask for it in the park or in the living room, and whether you ask for it or your husband does. Generalizing means that the same response is given even though the $S^D$s may vary somewhat.

Discrimination and generalization, taken together, result in stimulus control. These processes function on numerous aspects of the situation. A dog can be trained to discriminate the controlling verbal stimulus very precisely (i.e. he responds if and only if the command "roll over" is given, and not when you say "down" or "play dead" or "Timbuctu"). At the same time, the dog can be trained to generalize the response so that it occurs in different locations, for different people, and for different rewards. This is accomplished, once the basic response is acquired, through further training under different conditions, called "proofing" in dog training lingo.

It is usually important to incorporate generalization training into any program involving problem behavior. For instance, if you are dealing with a dog that is fearful of strangers, you want to address the problem in all the situations where strangers might be encountered. As the dog begins to accept strangers in one setting, a switch to a new setting should be introduced. A variety of different stimuli should be used. In this example, a number of different strangers would need to be included (males, females, children, etc.). Generalization is facilitated if new responses can be conditioned to stimuli that are common across different situations. The dog could be conditioned to approach an outstretched hand for treats - this is a stimulus that any stranger can present.

The extent to which an animal discriminates and generalizes can be measured by mapping out a *gradient of responding* (called a generalization gradient). Suppose your dog barks whenever he hears a doorbell. His barking would be most intense when he hears the sound of your own doorbell (called the training stimulus). If you collect a set of doorbells that vary in how similar they sound to the training doorbell, you can present the sound of these new doorbells to your dog and measure the intensity of his barking. Doorbells that are most similar in sound to the training doorbell will elicit barking that is almost as intense as it is for the training doorbell. As the doorbell sound becomes more and more different from the training

doorbell, the intensity of the barking declines. The gradient portrays the dog's natural generalization to doorbells. If you want him to only respond to

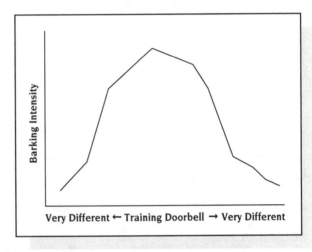

the training doorbell, it would be necessary to teach him to discriminate between your doorbell and other doorbells by rewarding him for responses to your doorbell only and/or punishing him for any response to other doorbells. This would steepen the generalization gradient.

## The Sit Test

In one of his American Kennel Gazette columns, Ian Dunbar describes a test of how well your dog is under stimulus control. Here's an example of what he talked about:

Assuming that your dog sit extremely reliably when you say "sit", try these command words. Remember to do everything else exactly the sameas you would if you were asking your dog to sit (stand the same, look at your dog the same, hold your hands the same, etc.).

1. "pit"       2. "kit"

3. "hit"       4. "spit"

5. "skit"      6. "shit"

7. "dork"      8. "spazz"

Without specific training, most dogs will respond by sitting to all these words, with the possible exception of 7 and sometimes, 8.

Another aspect of stimulus control is how well your dog ha come under control of your signal "sit" versus other features of the situation. Try changing these features. Ask your dog to sit while you lie on the ground, while you stand on your head, while you stand on the other side of a door, while you stand with your back to the door, while your dog is standing on a chair, while your dog is running alongside you, and so on and so forth. Some dogs deal with these tests very well, others do not.

## A Package of Stimuli

Often the dog will learn not only about the $S^D$ that you intend; he may also learn that other stimuli are important predictors as well. How many times have you seen a dog in the ring fall apart on the recall exercise because of the absence of extra signals from the handler? We call it body language. In training, the handler dips her head slightly or curves her body in such a way as to encourage a straight front. In the ring, the handler can't do this. She isn't aware that the dog considers this body language an integral part of the command and without it, the dog doesn't recognize what is being asked.

Imagine the dog that comes to your training school and is taught to sit during the first class. In all probability, the dog learns that *in* the context of the classroom, *while* the instructor is talking, *while* the dog is wearing a special new collar and leash, *while* the owner is bending over, holding the leash, speaking to the dog and waving a treat, he ought to sit in order to get that treat. The $S^D$ is actually a conglomeration of all these stimuli put together - a package of stimuli. Change something in the package and you may not get the response anymore because the new, slightly different stimulus does not yet control the response. In this example, remove the treat from the owner's hand and magically, the dog behaves as though he has never heard the word "sit" before. Ask the owner to stand up straight and the dog doesn't sit. Just changing the location can have the same effect: go home and the dog doesn't sit. As the weeks go on, however, the dog begins to hone in on the consistent stimuli and starts ignoring anything irrelevant.

Anyone who has proofed directed jumping for obedience, agility or flyball knows that the dog has to be systematically set up at every imaginable angle to go over the jump. And even if you teach the dog to go over the jump from a variety of angles in one direction, when you switch around and have the dog go over the jump in the other direction, all the training seems lost. That's because the stimulus package is different and the dog has to learn to generalize.

## Which Stimuli will the Dog Learn About?

All stimuli are not created equal. In other words, the dog will not necessarily pay equal attention to all the stimuli that are present. So you cannot assume that he will come under equal control of all the stimuli. That's why it really is okay to wear a new pair of shoes when training without the dog falling apart because the package is different. He may even notice the new shoes but he has learned from past experience that the shoes you wear are pretty much irrelevant to his life and so he doesn't attend to shoes. He is perfectly capable of learning to pay attention to your shoes if that is something you would desire. Theoretically, you could teach a dog that "sit" means sit when you are wearing your running shoes, that "sit" means to lie down when you are wearing your slippers, and that "sit" means run away when you are wearing your dress shoes. (If you are like me, "off" really only means "off" when I am wearing nice clothes!) As long as something is a relevant predictor of reinforcement, the dog will come under control of that stimulus. Many dogs learn to exhibit entirely different patterns of behavior, depending on the collar they are wearing: show ring collar, obedience collar, tracking harness, and so on. The key is predictability. As long as you are consistent in presenting a stimulus that predicts a particular response will be reinforced, the dog will come under its control.

## Salience and Overshadowing

The easiest way to ensure that your dog will learn the $S^D$ you intend is to make the stimulus very salient to the dog. For a dog, certain things, such as a piece of wiener moving around at eye level, is *really, really* salient. Touch is also very salient; so are loud sounds and smells. Remember, the dog will only learn about a stimulus if he perceives it and pays attention to it. In other words, you may give him an entire package of stimuli to learn but he may only pick up on the most salient elements. The less salient elements of the package will be *overshadowed* by the more salient elements. For example, if you are teaching a new behavior and using numerous cues, such as a physical prompt, a body movement, and a word, the dog will likely come to controlled primarily by one or two of these. Agility instructors demonstrate this all the time. Often students will be required to participate in an exercise where an entire course is run without uttering a single verbal command. Handlers usually balk at this but more often than not, the dog does as well, if not better than normal. Most agility dogs cue on the handler's body movements. If anything, verbal commands may interfere with the handler's inclination to provide clear body signals.

The way I teach a dog to "get it in" (to slide his butt into heel position) is a good example of what can happen with stimulus control. I usually teach this behavior by placing a collar around the dog's tummy, with a leash attached to it that I run behind my back and hold with my right hand. Then I say "get it in" and pull the dog's butt so it touches my left leg. Once the dog has experienced this a few times, I start to lessen the physical aid of pulling on the leash. Of course, initially the dog doesn't do anything because he hasn't yet acquired the response. Gradually, I pull less and less and eventually the dog offers the behavior as soon as I put tension on the lead. When I fade the tension out, the dog still responds. Now what stimulus controls the dog's behavior? It's always my body movement of preparing to tug on the leash. So this has to be gradually faded as well. Eventually, the behavior will come under the one stimulus that finally is the most salient: the words "get it in". (Refer to a later section on prompting and fading for a related discussion.)

So the moral of the story is: if you want your dog to rely on one specific cue (verbal, visual, etc.), gradually fade out all other controlling stimuli. If, out of the blue, you present just one element of the stimulus package, you can't expect the dog to give you the behavior. And if he doesn't, don't assume that he's being stubborn. The behavior simply isn't under the control of the stimulus that you are providing.

The fact that certain stimuli overshadow other stimuli is my explanation for why (this is my opinion and I wish there were scien-

tific data to support this) most dogs seem to learn the basic stationary commands (sit, down, stand) far more quickly with the lure-
reward method than with the more traditional method of physically
placing the dog. The body posturing and tactile contact involved
with physically placing the dog is so salient to the dog that these
stimuli seem to overshadow any verbal commands that are given at
the same time. It is difficult to fade out the prompts and retain any
learning at all to the verbal commands. At first, the handler still has
to bend over and touch the dog on the body, then the handler has to
bend over and reach for the dog, then bend over, and so on. Eventually, the dog begins to respond to the verbal stimulus and the
handler can wean off the remaining body movements.

With the lure-reward method, the dog seems to learn about both
the visual and verbal stimuli, although the visual element is still
more salient to the dog than the verbal. However, it is relatively easy
to fade out the visual cue by hiding the food in the hand, then
removing the food from the hand, then gradually moving the hand
less and less until the visual prompt is gone and all that remains is
the verbal stimulus. Because the lure-reward method is hands-off,
you avoid the difficulties of weaning off a tactile prompt which
seems to overshadow other component of the stimulus package.

## Blocking

Suppose you have trained your dog to go lie down whenever you
turn on the TV. Then you decide that you'd like him to learn to lie
down on command as well. So you say "lie down" at the same time
as the TV comes on. After the dog has experienced the words and the
TV together for awhile, you try the command alone. Guess what
happens. The dog will not lie down. Why? Because the command has
been *blocked* from learning. The dog has no reason to learn anything
about the words. He already knows what he needs to know from the
TV. Why would he even bother to pay attention to the words? Sure,
he probably hears them but he doesn't necessarily notice its asso-

ciation with lying down. He doesn't have to. The TV is there. There is
no need to learn redundant information.

Switching a dog from verbal signals to hand signals is an analogous situation. If your dog has learned to respond well to verbal
signals and you add in hand signals, theoretically, he will not learn
the new signals **if you present them together**. Rather than giving
him a redundant signal, it is better to structure the situation so that
the new signal provides the dog with information. If the new signal
tells the dog something, he will notice it and learn about it. This is
accomplished by simply presenting the new signal slightly *before* the
learned signal. If this is done consistently, the dog will learn that the
hand signal predicts the verbal signal. Once this is learned, the dog
will respond to the hand signal in anticipation of the verbal signal
(classical conditioning again). Then you can drop (or fade) the verbal
signal from the sequence.

Blocking is a frequent problem for agility trainers attempting to
teach "left" and "right" responses to their dogs. Typically, a trainer
will start the dog by giving plenty of body language to help him
choose the correct jump (out of a number of choices). If the dog is to
take the left jump, the handler might start by standing to the left of
the dog, command the dog to jump while running alongside, then
ducking off to the left, giving the command, and a visible arm movement toward the correct jump. Eventually, a lot of the extra movement is faded out. However, often the handler will continue to stay
on the side of the dog that is consistent with the turn, even though
when running a course, this may not be feasible. Unfortunately, the
majority of dogs pick up on the body language, which is very salient,
and never pick up on the verbal commands, which are blocked from
learning. Because the owner is already standing on the correct side,
why should the dog bother to learn the verbal command? The dog
continues to cue off the body. Then, when you decide to "test" how
reliable your dog is on the verbal command only, you are in for a
nasty surprise. You stand on the right side of the dog and command

"left", and sure enough, the dog turns right.

How should it be done? Well, you could stand on the right of the dog, command "left", and as he begins to move, cross behind to draw him left. Because your verbal command comes prior to your movement, there should be no blocking. He will learn that when you say "left", you are going to move left even though you are on his right when you give the command. Sounds easy, eh? Well, it's not always and I'll come back to this training issue a bit later.

## The Reliability of the $S^D$

The way to assess the reliability of the $S^D$ is to look at the strength of the association between the $S^D$ and the response-reinforcement relation. For instance, if the dog, after hearing the word "sit", always ends up in a sitting position, the stimulus "sit" is a highly predictable stimulus for the R (sit) → $S^{R+}$(cookie) relation. This is the reason for the maxim "Only give the command once". Every time the dog hears "sit" and he doesn't sit, you degrade the significance of the $S^D$ to the response-reinforcer.

The reliability of a stimulus can far outweigh the salience. Even a very subtle stimulus can be learned if it is the best predictor of the response-reinforcement connection. Remember Clever Hans and the stimuli he picked up on? His "counting" response came under the control of a stimulus so subtle that von Osten himself didn't know he was giving the cue. Because von Osten truly believed the horse was capable of arithmetic, these subtle cues were the only predictors that Hans could learn.

In an old magazine, I came across a description of a circus dog, a poodle named Munito, who could answer questions asked by the audience on topics relating to geography, botany, natural history, and mathematics. The dog would convey the answer by choosing a card from a large number of cards laid out on the floor. He answered each question by picking the card which displayed the correct answer. But what Munito was actually doing was circling the cards, appearing very thoughtful, but all the while waiting until he heard an almost inaudible (at least to the human ear), clicking noise made by his trainer with a fingernail or a toothpick. The noise cued the dog to pick up the card he was nearest. This apparently made for a very convincing performance!

The issue of reliability is why I dislike using the command word within the praise (i.e. "Good Sit", "Good Down", etc.). You are presenting the dog with an $S^D$ but he cannot perform the response because he is already sitting or lying down. Whenever you say "Good Sit" while your dog is sitting, you are contributing to the dog's understanding that, upon hearing "sit", he should do nothing.

For the same reason, I have trouble with handlers who tell their dogs to "sit" or "down" during the group exercises, *after* the dog is already sitting or lying down. The judge says "sit you dogs" and everyone looks at their dog and says "sit" even though there is absolutely no way that the dog could possibly sit any more than it is already doing.

My perspective on this is not necessarily true because what is really at issue here is this: "does the dog learn that 'sit' is an action or that 'sit' is a position?" If 'sit' is an action, then every time you say "sit", you want the dog to move into a sitting position. However, if 'sit' is a position, then it would be reasonable to praise with "good sit" because the dog is in the process of doing a sit. Any time this question is raised, it appears that people are pretty mixed on the answer. Some firmly believe 'sit' is an action while others believe it is a position. The only real evidence we have to consider is that a dog can acquire the response of sitting from a stand position extremely reliably and then not have a clue what to do when you command him to "sit" from a down position. Both of these actions have to be trained separately to the same command. In other words, when the dog hears "sit" and he is in a standing position, he learns to do action$_1$, when he is in a prone position, he learns to do action$_2$ in response to the exact same signal ("sit"). Similarly, a dog has to learn to lie down from a sit and to lie down from a stand; to stand up from a sit and to stand up from a down. This certainly leads me to think of the position commands as actions. For this reason, I do not use the command within praise or use the command when the dog is already in the position for maximal stimulus control (more reliable performance).

Of course, dogs are capable of discriminating a word given in a commanding voice and a word given in a praising voice, and so they learn to respond only to signals presented in a commanding voice. But why make it so tough? Use a reinforcer that is distinct from the S$^D$.

> "Then I went out for some Ziffs, they're exactly like Zuffs,
>
> But the Ziffs live on cliffs and the Zuffs live on bluffs.
>
> And, seeing how bluffs are exactly like cliffs,
>
> It's mighty hard telling the Zuffs from the Ziffs."
>
> Dr. Seuss

## Context Effects

The context in which learning occurs can affect learning and performance dramatically. The context becomes a part of the stimulus package, just like anything else. Obedience competitors often engage in a set of rituals before going in the ring which serves to cue the dog that this is the appropriate context for obedience exercises, rewards, and corrections. I always say to my dogs "It's time to work" and I give them a piece of whatever food reward I am using (my jumpstart). This signals to the dog that this particular reinforcement is now available, and signals that the context is now appropriate for obedience and that he ought to be "on his toes".

Anything that signals to the animal that certain contingencies are in effect is also called an *occasion setter*. The animal learns something different about occasion setters than he does about other aspects of the stimulus package. For example, when Pavlov's dog heard a metronome, it is thought that somehow a representation of food was conjured up in his brain. The sound of the metronome became a CS and when the dog heard it, he began to salivate, which was a CR. However, when Pavlov's dog entered the laboratory, it is thought that somehow a representation of the association between the sound of the metronome and food was conjured up. The laboratory set the occasion for this association rather than serving as a CS itself. Entering the laboratory did not cause the dog to salivate but it did cause the dog to be ready to salivate as soon as he heard a metronome. It is as though responding was facilitated because the animal was in the appropriate context. In a different context altogether, the dog may not have even salivated to the metronome. We all know that a well-trained obedience dog can show a very sluggish response if you ask him to perform "cold". It's the same kind of thing. You haven't set the occasion for responding.

Occasion setters also do not undergo extinction in the same way as does a CS (see next section). Pavlov's dogs could have gone into the laboratory several times a day, without hearing the metronome or receiving food, and still the faciliatory effect of the context would not extinguish.

## What about Teaching a Discrimination?

Thus far, I've been talking about dogs learning a discrimination between a command or cue and the lack of a command or cue. In other words, run out and fetch the dumbell when I say "get it" and don't when I don't ask for it. That's a simple discrimination. But what about teaching the dog to respond in one way to one $S^D$ and a different way to a different $S^D$? This is a complex discrimination.

In the psychology laboratory, the standard method for teaching an animal a discrimination is to reward one type of response and ignore responses to other stimuli. For instance, say you are training a pigeon to peck at a green circle when it appears on the screen and not to peck at a red circle when it appears on the screen. The circles are not always in the same place (otherwise, the pigeon would not attend to the color at all but would instead learn the location of the correct circle to peck - spatial location is almost always easier to learn than any other attribute). If the bird has already been trained to peck at circles, he will start out pecking at both circles. If you consistently reward pecks to the green and never reward pecks to the red, eventually pecks at the red circle will dwindle. The green circle becomes an excitatory $S^D$ (called an $S^+$) because it signals the response-reward contingency. The red circle becomes an inhibitory $S^D$ (called an $S^-$) because it signals the *lack of* a response-reward contingency.

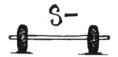

Likewise, suppose you want your dog to retrieve your slippers from a closet containing a few pairs of footwear. Provided your dog already possesses a retrieve response, the easiest method (from a trainer's perspective) would be to send the dog to your closet to retrieve. You would then reward him for bringing slippers and ignore him whenever he brings anything else. Theoretically, over time, the dog will come to bring only your slippers. The slippers will become an $S^+$ and other shoes ($S^-$) will come to inhibit the retrieving response.

Dogs that are being trained to detect accelerants at fire sites often go through a tough discrimination in the beginning. Apparently dogs that are trained to detect the odor of gasoline also respond to the odor of burnt carpet and various other substances that are common at fire sites. Presumably these burnt substances all share some chemical component to which the dogs initially pay attention. It takes further discrimination training for the dogs to learn to inhibit responding to the non-accelerant odors by becoming $S^-$s.

### Is there a more efficient way?

The procedure described above is easy for the trainer, but not for the animal. The pigeon will peck at the red circle many, many times before learning the discrimination. The dog's retrieve response may well extinguish if he chooses the incorrect shoes too many times. Certainly, the animal will experience a great deal of frustration.

In some cases, the animal may not be motivated to avoid incorrect responses, if the cost is relatively small. In most cases, an incorrect response just means that reinforcement is delayed until they can respond again. In an early attempt to teach Ciaran a left-right discrimination, I set him up in a hallway that ended in a choice between a hallway to the left and a hallway to the right. I randomly baited either the left or the right hallway with food, told him to "go", and just before he reached the choice point, I gave him the appropriate "left" or "right" command. Whenever he made an error, we repeated the trial until he succeeded (called correction trials). Over a series of several sessions, I ran Ciaran for approximately 500 trials and his performance was essentially random. He adopted a strategy of "choose whichever hallway had been baited last time". He showed no evidence of learning at all and I can only assume that the cost of making an incorrect choice was not at all aversive and consequently, he was not motivated to pick up on the stimuli I wanted him to learn about[6].

Is there a way to make learning easier? One simple technique would be to incorporate different reinforcers for the different responses. For instance, if I had baited the left hallway with chicken and the right hallway with beef (assuming Ciaran likes both equally well), I could have aided Ciaran's learning of the discrimination (this is called the *differential outcomes effect*). Alternatively, I could have delivered a mild punisher whenever Ciaran chose the wrong hallway, and the discrimination between the choices might be learned more rapidly. However, then the incorrect choice on any one trial (the S) would elicit not only frustration, but anxiety as well. In one study, researchers usedthis type of procedure to teach dogs to discriminate between the odor of an explosive (S+) and the odor of clean air (S). The dog was punished with a mild shock to the foot if he pressed the lever in the presence of clean air. The dogs became so stressed about the whole experiment that they couldn't perform well at all. As an analogy, imagine you are in school and on test day, your teacher hovers over you, ready to whack you with a ruler if you make a mistake. You'd hardly be able to concentrate on the questions very well, would you? I did try this with Ciaran in a separate training effort. I set him up with a jump to the left and a jump to the right. If he chose the right jump after I commanded "left", I would toss my keys at him (a serious conditioned aversive stimulus for him - the keys have been conditioned unintentionally as they occasionally fall on his head as I try to get the front door open!). This made him totally lose it and he refused to jump at all after the second or third

---

[6] Also, many animals have what is called a "win-stay" strategy. This means that in a choice situation, they tend to respond whichever way paid off the last time. For most species this makes sense because they tend to find their food in the same places. Wolves tend to find rabbits near warren and deer near resting or feeding areas. Prey are not distributed around the wolf's world in a random fashion.

error. That technique was quickly ruled out!

With this in mind, consider one of the traditional methods of teaching the utility scent discrimination exercise. First, assume that your dog is already trained to the point that if you say "find it", he's learned he is supposed to come back with an article. Then, place two articles on the floor with one tied down and tell him to "find it". What will happen? The dog will run out and roughly 50% of the time he will attempt to pick up the one that is tied down. I expect the inability to retrieve the tied-down article is mildly aversive, at least to an avid retriever or a force-retrieve trained dog, and so the tied-down article quickly becomes an S⁻. He knows he needs to retrieve something and he can't pick the thing up. He gets frustrated and pulls at it or he gives up. Eventually, he learns to check for which article is tied down. He might do this by looking for the fishing line or he might learn to nudge the article first to see if it is attached. In some cases, he might actually notice that the article that isn't attached seems to have a stronger smell. That's the basic difference between quick and slow learners - some dogs are more likely to notice the association of smell and correct article right away, while other dogs learn other predictors (such as which articles have ties attached). With the dogs that don't notice the difference in smell right away, you then have to go about systematically making these other stimuli less relevant (i.e. loose ties, etc.). Eventually, the dog is conditioned to retrieve the smelly article and to ignore the non-smelly article. Then you begin adding more non-smelly articles. Suddenly there are more aversive S⁻s. The dog has a number of alternatives out there and all of them are wrong except one. Just a bit stressful, eh?

### Errorless Discrimination Learning

There is a better way. Herb Terrace wanted to know if animals <u>had</u> to make errors in order to learn a right-wrong discrimination. Does the dog just learn to retrieve the smelly article (excitatory conditioning) or does the dog just learn to inhibit retrieving the non-smelly articles (inhibitory conditioning) or does the dog learn both things - to retrieve the smelly one and to avoid the non-smelly ones (both excitatory and inhibitory). Any of these possibilities would get the job done but knowing what is necessary for learning tells us what we need to teach.

Terrace developed a procedure called errorless discrimination learning that involves only excitatory conditioning. If we go back to the pigeon example, imagine that whenever the green circle comes on, the circle is large and very bright and very green. Next imagine that when the red circle comes on, it is small and not very red and blends in with the background. Obviously the pigeon would notice the green circle and peck at it. It wouldn't be likely to peck at the red key because he probably wouldn't notice it. After much experience with this, so that the bird is always pecking green and never pecking red, suppose you ever-so-gradually started making the red circle a bit large and more red. Terrace's research showed, if the procedure is sufficiently gradual, the pigeon doesn't even notice the red circle and continues to peck only at the green. In the end, both keys are of equal size, brightness, and intensity of color. The bird may make an odd error here and there but for the most part, the discrimination is learned and the bird rarely responds to the incorrect stimulus.

What is especially interesting is that the birds in Terrace's procedure showed no aversion to the S⁻. They never tried to avoid the red circle nor did they show any frustration or anxiety about the procedure. Terrace proved that making mistakes is not a necessary component of learning a right-wrong discrimination.

## Can Dogs Learn Scent Discrimination With an Errorless Procedure?

Back in October 1989, *Off-Lead* published an article entitled *The sweet smell of success (an alternative approach to teaching the scent articles)*, written by Lonnie Morgan. In it, she describes an excellent approximation to an errorless procedure. I'll describe what is essentially Morgan's procedure, with slight modifications.

Initially, the dog is asked to retrieve a thrown smelly article (throwing it makes it very salient to the dog). The article smells of meat (I use slightly-gone-off chicken liver because it is extremely smelly and gooey so it sticks well). At the same time, there is a non-smelly article sitting on the floor, several feet away. Over many, many trials, the smelly article is made a bit less salient (throwing fades to tossing and tossing fades to placing and placing fades to the article just sitting there when the trial starts), while at the same time, the other article is moved ever so gradually closer and closer to the place where the smelly article is. In addition, the meaty smell on the article is gradually mixed with the trainer's smell. I start by rubbing gooey chicken liver on the article, then I rub gooey liver on my hand and then rub my hand on the article, then I gradually put less and less liver on my hand, then I just scent the article with my hand. Additional articles can be added in as you progress, always starting with a new one a few feet away and gradually moving it closer. If the dog should happen to pick up the wrong article, the worst that happens is he gets no reward. Because it happens so rarely, if at all, the dog should show little anxiety. Whenever the smelly article is moved to a new location in the pile, pull the others away a bit to make the correct article salient. Then, on the next trial, keep the smelly article in the same position but pull the other articles in close again. Dogs that are taught in this manner can learn scent discrimination in no time, as compared to the tie-down method. Learning is rapid because the smell is the most salient and predictable stimulus for the dog to rely on and because incorrect choices, and hence frustration, are so infrequent.

## Preparedness

At first, it was thought that as long as two stimuli went together, so that one signaled the other, you would get classical conditioning. It shouldn't matter what the stimuli are. But this is not the case. It is easier to associate certain types of CSs with certain UCSs. We know this from Garcia and Koelling (1966), who designed a very clever experiment using "bright, noisy, tasty" water. They trained rats to drink water which was flavored (tasty) and whenever the rat drank from the tube, a light flashed and a clicker sounded (bright and noisy). This is called a *compound stimulus* because the stimulus is made up of several elements. Although usually the animals had normal water, whenever they were given this wierd water to drink, it was a signal for an aversive event. One group of rats experienced shock to their feet when they drank the water, while the other group was injected with lithium chloride, which made them very ill. After a few pairings of these two events, the researchers offered the rats *either* bright, noisy water *or* tasty water. What they found was that the rats associated the flavor of the water with illness, but not with shock, and they associated the auditory and visual stimuli (the light and the clicker) with shock but not with illness. There are many similar examples of selectivity in learning - it is as though animals come *prepared* to make certain types of associations. To a rat, things you eat or drink may make you sick but they don't usually inflict pain. Things that make noises or flash at you are more likely to hurt you than make you sick. The tendency to associate certain types of stimuli more readily than others is called *preparedness*. This is a special problem faced by people (and animals) undergoing chemo-therapy. The chemo makes them ill but the association is made between whatever food they were eating and the illness, not the medical treatment. This happens even though the person is aware of what is causing the illness. Similarly, my father, who had smoked for thirty years, contracted pneumonia and felt extremely ill whenever he lit up. Despite the fact that he knows it was the pneumonia and not the cigarettes that made him feel sick, he has not been able to touch a cigarette for several years now. Just the thought of lighting up makes him nauseous (everyone in the family is thrilled except him - he enjoyed smoking!).

Preparedness can influence what stimuli an animal associates with a response or the ease with which an animal can learn about stimuli. In one study, dogs were taught to perform two responses. One response was to lift a front leg up and down repeatedly in quick succession. The other response was to lift a front leg up and hold it for approximately ten seconds. For one group of dogs, the signal to perform the up-and-down response was a pulsed tone that went on and off, on and off. The signal to perform the lift-leg-and-hold response was a continuous tone that stayed on for approximately ten seconds. These dogs learned the discrimination easily. The dogs in the second group had the signals reversed. When they heard the pulsed noise, they were to lift and hold the leg. When they heard the constant noise, they were to lift the leg up and down. The dogs in this group found it extremely difficult to learn the discrimination. For the first group, it was as though the stimuli and responses went together and this made it easier for the dogs to learn the associations.

Patricia McConnell, Ph.D. of Dog's Best Friend in Black Earth, Wisconsin was so interested in the nature of S$^D$s that she made this the topic of her Ph.D. dissertation work. She analyzed the sound patterns of the commands used by shepherds controlling the behavior of their Border Collies while working stock. She found that, regardless of the country of origin and the language of the shepherd, the commands they used for specific behaviors were very similar. They tended to use short, rapidly repeating, rising notes for commands which increased the dog's activity and long, continuous, descending notes for commands which decreased the dog's activity. Coincidence or what? Well, Trisha then created arbitrary sounds that matched these same patterns and played the sounds to Border

Collie puppies at various times of the day. Sure enough, when the puppies heard the low, continuous noise, they tended to settle down and when they heard the short rising noise, they tended to move around. This suggests that dogs are somehow genetically pro-grammed or *predisposed* to behave in certain ways to certain stimuli. I guess it is no surprise that when we want a dog to come, we squeak out "come, come, come" in a high-pitched voice and when we want a dog to stay, we croon "stay" in a low voice. We're giving them an added advantage for success. So it's really true even for dogs: "it's not what you say but how you say it"!

## Discrimination or Reflexive Behavior?

I want to come back to the discussion of teaching left-right direc-tional commands to agility dogs. The majority of dogs that I have seen who appear to respond reasonably consistently to "left" and "right" regardless of the handler's position (realize that if you're only about 50% correct, your dog is either behaving randomly or he has a bias to consistently turn either left or right), have been trained to respond to the commands more as reflexes than as performing a discrimination. Let me explain the training procedure (courtesy of Linda Mecklenberg, DVM of Columbus, Ohio). You start by teaching the dog to turn left (or right, it doesn't matter which comes first) whenever he hears the word "left" (throw a ball or food in that direction). You do this over and over again a million times, gradually working your way around to be in various positions (facing the dog, behind the dog, on either side of the dog, stationary or running, with and without obstacles). When the dog is performing reasonably consistently in that you always get a body movement to the left when you say "left", you stop training left and start training right. You do the same thing. Command "right" and induce the dog to turn right a million times until it essentially becomes a reflexive action that is elicited whenever the dog hears the word "right". Only then do you begin intermixing the two commands. Because only one stimulus-response association is taught at a time, the dog is really not learning a discrimination between two alternatives. It is more like the dog is learning two very specific and independent stimulus-response units. This is a far simpler form of learning because 'left' elicits turning the body to the left and 'right' elicits turning the body to the right rather than if 'left' turn to the left and if 'right' turn to the right. Although we know that dogs can learn the latter, it may be more efficient and easier for them to learn the former (in other words, it takes a lot less brainpower to learn two simple relationships than it does to learn a rule for a discrimination between two choices).

## Learning Sets

The distinction between simple and complex learning relates to the learning set research. A "learning set" refers to the notion that an animal can learn rules for responding if taught in a certain way. In a typical learning set experiment, a dog sits behind a barrier and a tray containing an object is pushed into his view. The dog looks at the object and then it is removed. A few seconds later, the tray is pushed back and two objects are available, one is the object the dog saw a few seconds earlier, the other is a different object. If we are trying to teach the dog *matching-to-sample*, he is supposed to choose the object he saw before (he is supposed to match his choice to the sample he saw earlier). If we are trying to teach the dog ***nonmatching-to-sample***, he is supposed to choose the object he **did not** see before. Now, if you use the same sets of objects, say 10 pairs that are always presented together, the dog could very easily learn each specific pair. If matching-to-sample: "when I see a teddy bear, I choose the teddy bear"; "when I see the dog bowl, I choose the dog bowl". If nonmatching-to-sample: "when I see a teddy bear, I choose the Frisbee"; "when I see the dog bowl, I choose the squeaky toy". And so on for all ten pairs. Alternatively, the dog could learn a specific rule. If matching-to-sample: "when I see x, choose x". If nonmatching-to-sample: "when I see x, choose y". The dog is considered to have developed a learning set when he has achieved a rule for making the discrimination. You can determine this by offering novel pairs of items. If the dog can make the correct choice the first time he is faced with new objects, he has developed a learning set. He can also learn to reverse the learning set by switching him from, say, matching-to-sample to nonmatching-to-sample. At first, he'll make tons of mistakes but eventually he will learn the new rule. Then you switch him back. Again, loads of errors but he manages. With a lot of training, you can switch and he will make only one error, which tells him the rule has changed and he will adjust. Pretty cool.

Some dog trainers should worry about this learning set stuff. Detection dogs are often trained with very specific stimuli. If they are destined to be airport dogs, they are offered choices between a drug and the usual sorts of things found in luggage: shaving cream, lotion, shampoo, toothpaste, etc. If the trainers are really consistent, the dogs might well learn "choose the odd smell, the non-perfume smell" rather than "choose the heroin smell". It isn't a very likely scenario but it is possible.

The main reason I bring up learning sets is because I think some dogs do acquire learning sets and a specific example is described in the later section on shaping.

## Experimental Neuroses

I want to mention experimental neuroses in case you ever might be in the position to diagnose such a bizarre behavior. Experimental neuroses refers to the outcome of a procedure in which an animal is forced to perform a discrimination that is no longer possible. I will provide a laboratory explanation first and then a real-life example.

In this study, dogs were required to discriminate between a circle and an ellipse. One group of dogs had to respond to one and not the other. For the other group, it was the reverse. They were rewarded with food for responding correctly and the lights were turned off for a brief time for responding incorrectly. After the dogs learned this task, the circle was made ever-so-slightly elliptical and the ellipse was made ever-so-slightly circular. The dogs were still able to make the discrimination most of the time. Several times, the stimuli were changed so as to become slightly more similar. Eventually the dogs were unable to tell the two stimuli apart. You might expect that they would simply stop responding or respond randomly. Instead, they began to whine and bark, pace and pant nervously, and try to escape from the chamber. They showed a great deal of distress. Even more strange, when they were again presented with the **original** stimuli, the circle and the ellipse, they could no longer perform the discrimination. This bizarre effect was labeled experimental neuroses.

Several years ago someone told me a story of a police dog that had been trained to attack on command. It was also trained with a "built-in off switch" - if the suspect raised his arms, the dog was to let go and back off, without any direct command from the officer. This seemed like a good idea until the night the team was searching a warehouse for a suspected criminal. When they came upon the fellow, both the dog and the officer went for him. Desperate, the suspect grabbed a chair and wielded it above his head to threaten the officer. In the act of raising the chair, the suspect's arms were also raised. This was the dog's cue not to attack. However, everything else about the situation was telling the dog to attack. Instead, the dog began to circle, pace, and whine. While I have no idea what happened to the officer, several months later the dog was still circling and whining. It would continue the behavior incessantly unless physically prevented. The dog had blown a fuse and was suffering from real-life experimental neuroses.

The take-home message from this story? Don't give your dog incompatible signals, like "sit down". He might just show you that he is under incredible stimulus control!

# Extinction

## Is Extinction Unlearning?

What happens when you stop providing reinforcement for a behavior? This is called *extinction*. Extinction involves the removal of reinforcement. In classical conditioning, the association between the CS and the UCS is degraded. The CS is presented without the UCS (for Pavlov's dogs, the metronome sounds but no food is delivered). In instrumental conditioning, the response is no longer reinforced (the $S^D$ is presented and the response occurs but nothing happens to reinforce the response). In both types of conditioning, responding gradually declines. In both types of conditioning, the animal actually learns the new *lack* of relationship between the CS and the UCS or between the response and reinforcement. In other words, new learning occurs - they don't *unlearn* what they had learned previously.

When you put a behavior on extinction, the first thing you will notice is that the animal gets very anxious and frustrated. Because the animal is accustomed to receiving reinforcement in this situation, the animal gets aroused when this is no longer forthcoming. Over time, the likelihood of seeing the response declines. However, there will be occasional bursts of responding, called *extinction bursts*.

This behavior is presumably motivated by the frustration. For example, if your dog paws at you for attention and you decide to extinguish this behavior by no longer attending to him, your dog will probably become agitated, start whining, and try to paw you even harder. Sometimes a dog will even become aggressive toward the owner. Once the behavior finally drops off (this could take as long as an hour or two) and you take a break from the dog for awhile, you should expect to go through the same experience again when you return. This is called *spontaneous recovery*. The bursts might be less intense the second time. During the initial phases of extinction, anytime the animal is not exposed to the CS or to the $S^D$ for awhile and then is re- exposed, you should expect to see a brief bout of responding. Gradually, the bursts and spontaneous recoveries become shorter and less frequent until finally responding ceases altogether when the animal is presented with the CS or the $S^D$. At this point, the behavior has extinguished.

As an aside, it is important to realize that you get spontaneous recovery of a learned behavior even if it has been punished. This is very useful because occasionally something terrible happens at just the wrong time. For instance, you are trying to speed up the turn on a retrieve and want to give a leash correction just after the pick up but instead you time it poorly and correct the dog *before* he picks up the object. The next time you send your dog to retrieve he avoids the object altogether. Or you release your dog on a flyball run and he is bulldozed by the dog on the opposing team. On the next run he refuses to go down to the box. In these cases, it is best not to get back up on the horse. That's our typical philosophy - work the dog through the problem as quickly as possible. Why? Just forget about training for the rest of the day and try again the next. Spontaneous recovery will kick in and the problem will have disappeared all by itself. Remember, though, that spontaneous recovery only works with behaviors that are well-learned - not new behaviors that really haven't been acquired yet.

## The Partial Reinforcement Extinction Effect

Another important feature of extinction is that the process is affected by the type of reinforcement schedule that had been in effect prior to extinction. The previous schedule determines the speed at which responding extinguishes and the level of frustration the animal experiences.

If the animal was maintained on a CRF schedule, in which every response is rewarded, a switch to extinction is extremely frustrating for the animal. The animal notices right away that the contingencies have changed and although the response disappears rapidly, this is accompanied by extreme arousal.

If the animal was maintained on an intermittent or differential schedule (in which only some responses are rewarded), an interesting thing happens when switched to an extinction procedure. The animal shows less frustrating and continues to respond for long periods, despite the fact that no responses are rewarded. This happens for two reasons. First, it is less obvious to the animal that the contingencies have changed because the change from partial to no reinforcement is not as drastic as a change from continuous to no reinforcement. Second, the animal is already accustomed to not receiving a reward for responding. This is called the *partial reinforcement extinction effect* (PREE). The persistence with which some animals will continue to respond, despite never being reinforced, can be quite surprising.

The PREE is bad news for dog owners. Often problem behavior is maintained on a partial schedule of reinforcement. The dog that whines to be released from his crate, for example, is probably on some sort of duration schedule. The longer the dog continues to whine, the more likely the owner will relent and release him. An extinction procedure for this type of problem is very easy for dog owners to understand and it takes no special training skills to implement. It does take an iron will, however. If you, as a trainer, recommend that the owner stop rewarding the whining behavior by leaving the dog in the crate until the whining stops, you had better warn the owner about the persistence. The dog has been conditioned to keep whining because in the past, the owner has always relented (eventually). Don't forget to also warn the owner about extinction bursts (you would expect intense periods of whining) and about spontaneous recovery (you would expect to go through a period of whining each time the dog is placed in the crate for some time, as well as if someone else, like the baby sitter, puts the dog in the crate, if the crate is moved to a new location, if the dog is placed in a crate at an unusual time of the day, and so on). These side effects will eventually disappear. But the side effects do tend to reduce the usefulness of an extinction procedure because owners find it difficult to live through it without breaking down.

It would seem, though, that if you switched the dog to a continuous reinforcement schedule for a time before instituting an extinction procedure, you should be able to eliminate the PREE. In other words, if you find you have been intermittently rewarding the dog for begging at the table, switch to reinforcing the begging response every time it occurs and then, cut the dog off cold turkey. Unfortunately, it doesn't work that way. Once a particular behavior has been on an intermittent schedule for any length of time, you can't erase the PREE effect. The animal has learned to continue responding even in the face of nonreinforcement and this learning stays with the animal, despite the shift to continuous reinforcement.

On the other hand, the PREE is very useful for maintaining responding when reinforcements are unavailable. The obedience ring is a good example. Although you are permitted to use some conditioned reinforcers in the ring, any use of food reinforcement or aversive consequences (corrections) are not allowed. Some dogs learn the relationship between the obedience ring and the lack of consequences very quickly (they are known as "ring-wise" dogs). However, you can make this discrimination less obvious to the dog simply by ensuring his performance is maintained on an intermittent schedule prior to trialing (that would have to be for both positive consequences <u>and</u> aversive consequences so the trialing and training situations are difficult to distinguish). Then, when he encounters the obedience ring, which, in essence, is like a session of extinction, you can benefit from the PREE. He is used to not always being rewarded for every response or corrected for every erroneous response and so he continues to respond in the ring, even though the consequences are lacking.

There is no evidence that the PREE holds for classically conditioned responses. If the CS is presented without the UCS, the conditioned response to the CS gradually disappears. If the pairings had been intermittent prior to the extinction procedure, the conditioning was not as strong anyway and so the CR disappears more quickly. An exception to this is the conditioned emotional response (CER) - a CER can be very resistant to extinction (to be covered in a later section).

# Aversive Control of Behavior

The use of aversive stimuli warrants a special discussion for three reasons. First, exposing an animal to aversive stimulation produces emotional side-effects that influence the learning process. Second, slight changes in procedure can have dramatic effects of the rate and extent of learning. And third, you can make a lot of mistakes using positive stimuli, such as food, and the worst thing that happens is you might have a skinny or an overweight dog. If you screw up with aversive stimuli, your dog gets traumatized and/or hurt. It is your responsibility to make sure you know exactly what you are doing if you decide to use aversive consequences.

With operant conditioning, aversive stimuli are used in both negative reinforcement and positive punishment procedures. In negative reinforcement, the aversive stimulus is presented until the animal performs the desired response, which is reinforced by ending the unpleasantness. Thus, the response increases in likelihood. In positive punishment, the aversive stimulus is presented when the animal performs the response. The response decreases in likelihood. I discuss each of these procedures in turn.

## NEGATIVE REINFORCEMENT

Negative reinforcement involves a negative contingency between the response and an aversive event. The response is often called an *escape/avoidance response*. There are several good examples of negative reinforcement from the world of humans. The mother who gives into her screaming child and buys him a candy bar is reinforced when the screaming stops. The next time the mother finds herself in the same situation, she is more likely to buy the child a candy right away to avoid the screaming altogether. The driver who hates seat belts but buckles up as soon as she starts the car in order to avoid the racket of the buzzer if she doesn't. The horse who feels his neck and mouth being pulled in one direction by the rider turns his body in that direction as a way to turn off the pressure.

Similarly, we are often negatively reinforced when dealing with our dogs. Guests come over and the dog starts acting up for attention. Rather than make a scene, we give the dog something to do. This serves to positively reinforce the dog's antics and at the same time, negatively reinforce the owner's behavior because the dog's annoying behavior stops. It is a vicious cycle.

In the laboratory two types of escape/avoidance procedures have been studied. In both *signaled* and *unsignaled* procedures, the most common setup is to place an animal in a shuttle box. A shuttle box has two compartments and the animal can move freely between them. In the signaled procedure, a signal comes on to warn the animal that an unpleasant event is imminent if the animal does not respond. Shortly after the warning signal, the animal is shocked. In most lab studies, the nasty stimulus is a shock but it could also be a blast of air, a spray of water, a loud noise, whatever. The animal can turn off the shock by shuttling from one side of the box to the other. If he waits until the shock comes on before moving to the other side, he has performed an escape response (he escapes the shock by moving to the other side). If he moves to the other side of the box during the warning signal, he avoids the shock altogether. This is an avoidance response. Once the animal learns the routine, he usually avoids virtually all the shocks. In the unsignaled procedure, everything is the same except that no warning signal is presented. The shocks are presented at regular intervals and so the animal learns to shuttle back and forth periodically in order to avoid the shocks. Unsignaled avoidance always takes longer to learn and rarely is the animal able to avoid all the shocks.

During the early stages of learning, the animal escapes rather than avoids the shocks. After a few repetitions, though, the animal starts to avoid the shocks altogether. The early stages of learning are also characterized by anxiety and stress because the animal is frequently shocked. Once the animal has learned the routine of avoiding the shocks, all signs of fear disappear.

**At First:   Warning → Shock**

**Escape Learning:   Warning → Shock → Response → Shock Off**

**Avoidance Learning:  Warning → Response → Warning Off/No Shock**

One key difference between negative reinforcement and punishment is that with negative reinforcement, the aversive stimulus is presented regardless of the animal's behavior. The seat belt buzzer comes on as soon as you start the car. The car doesn't care if you were planning to put your seat belt on or even if you were in the process already. The buzzer comes on anyway. The aversive stimulus is not contingent upon any behavior. Only turning it off is contingent upon a behavior. You can turn the buzzer off by putting the seat belt on. Similarly, with the horse example, the rider does not pull on the rein to punish the horse's behavior. The rider pulls on the rein to create an aversive stimulus that motivates the horse to turn in that direction. The horse is then reinforced for turning in that direction because it serves to remove the aversive pressure. With punishment, the aversive stimulus is presented contingently upon some unde-sired behavior. You make an unsafe lane change and your car is hit from behind. That's punishment. To make things more sticky, nega-tive reinforcement and punishment are usually used in conjunction. The aversive stimulus is presented, contingent upon some misbehavior (or lack of response), and it can then be escaped by performing the correct behavior.

Training a dog not to pull on the leash can be taught through an escape/avoidance/punishment procedure. With a signaled procedure, the owner gives the dog a warning (i.e. "easy") that he is about to reach the end of the leash. If the dog continues at the same speed, the owner jerks on the leash in such a way that the dog finds it unpleasant (punishment). The dog can then escape the jerking by slowing down (escape - negative reinforcement). However, if the dog slows down in response to the warning signal, he can avoid the leash jerks altogether (avoidance - negative reinforcement). Eventually, *if the jerking is sufficiently averse*, the dog will learn to slow down in response to the warning (this procedure doesn't usually work because the rewards of pulling far outweigh the aversiveness of a jerk on the leash).

A product called the Happy Walker is designed to beep when the dog puts pressure on the end of the leash. The noise, by itself, probably would not deter the average dog but the noise can serve as an automatic warning signal if it is consistently followed by a jerk on the leash if the dog does not slow down.

More often than not, dog owners attempt to teach the dog not to pull on the leash using an unsignaled procedure. The dog comes into contact with the leash jerks whenever he moves out of a defined range around the owner (depending on the length of the leash). In order to avoid the jerks, the dog must periodically slow down to ensure that it does not exceed the acceptable range. Obviously, this is a more difficult discrimination for the dog to learn than responding to a warning signal.

The "ear pinch" technique for teaching the retrieve is a negative reinforcement procedure. When done properly (i.e., as pure negative reinforcement rather than a combination of punishment and negative reinforcement), it can be an extremely effective method. The dog is presented with the dumbbell and told to "take it" (the warning signal). At first, he instantly receives a pinch to the ear that causes him to yelp (the pinch is the noncontingent aversive stimulus - it is noncontingent because the dog has no idea what "take it" means and so can't possibly be expected to perform the correct response). The yelping produces an open mouth into which the trainer can insert the dumbbell, at which time the pinch is *immediately* released. Timing is of the utmost importance. This procedure forces the dog to perform the escape response. With repetitions, the dog comes to recognize the "take it" warning signal and grabs the dumbbell before the trainer has the opportunity to pinch his ear. Trainers run into problems with this technique if the dog learns to avoid the pinch by pulling away from the trainer. Janice DeMello advocates a method for avoiding this potential problem: she recommends that the trainer constantly rub the dog's ear gently so 90% of the time, the stimulation on the ear is pleasant and so the dog is less inclined to pull away. Also, the trainer already has her hand on the dog's ear rather than reaching for it when the dog fails to take the dumbbell. When implemented properly, the dog should experience no more than a few pinches. If the trainer finds that she has fallen into the routine of constantly threatening the dog with a pinch, she is no longer using a negative reinforcement procedure. Instead, it has become an ineffective punishment procedure (punishment because it is contingent upon the dog not retrieving the dumbbell and ineffective because the dog has learned to "test" the situation to see what contingencies are in place).

Obedience trainers often use a form of escape/avoidance conditioning when they teach a dog to perform quickly. For instance, to teach the dog to respond quickly to the "down" command, the command is given and the leash is popped downward almost simultaneously. The pop is the aversive stimulus and it is presented noncontingently because there is no physical way the dog could respond simultaneously with the command. The goal is to teach the dog to find some way of anticipating the pop though. To teach the dog to get up quickly on the "heel" command, the command is given and the leash is popped in a forward direction almost simultaneously. I used to call these "noncontingent corrections" but really it is a straightforward example of using negative reinforcement. The command is given, the aversive stimulus is presented, and then removed as soon as the dog complies. The dog begins to respond more and more quickly to avoid the aversive stimulus. After a few trials, you end up with a very speedy response.

## Electronic Collars and Avoidance Responding

The remotely-controlled Tritronics electronic collar was designed with escape/avoidance responding in mind (Tortora, 1983). The dog is given the warning signal (i.e. "come"). If he turns and comes immediately, he avoids a shock. If he does not, he is shocked. When he responds, the shock is turned off. The only difference between this scenario and the laboratory shuttle box is that in the shuttle box, there are very few options for the dog. Initially, before he has learned the correct response, if he moves at all when shocked, he will very likely move to the other side. In the real world of training a dog to recall using an electronic collar, the trainer must also ensure that the dog very likely performs the response when shocked. Fortunately, many dogs do naturally run to the owner when frightened or hurt. Unfortunately, some do not and these dogs must be initially trained with a long line to ensure they do perform the correct response to turn off the shock. With consistent, sensitive training, a dog trained to recall with the aid of an electronic collar will exhibit no fear or anxiety because he *knows* exactly what he needs to do to avoid the shock. This technique is definitely not for everyone because it takes an unemotional trainer and exquisite timing to implement effectively. The dog may experience numerous shocks during the initial stages of training. Once he has learned the response, he rarely or never experiences shock again.

The real beauty of avoidance responding is that once the animal has learned the respond in order to avoid the aversive stimulus, he is extremely persistent. Think about it - once the animal is reliably avoiding the shock, he is never shocked. If he is never shocked, the response should gradually extinguish, right? But it doesn't. The animal keeps right on avoiding. You could take the collar off and throw it in the river and he will continue to avoid the shock (*provided you first ensured he learned the irrelevance of the collar itself*). What maintains the behavior? How can a shock, which is never experienced (because it is avoided) provide a source of motivation? It is thought that the avoidance response is positively reinforced through a reduction in fear associated with performing the response and with turning off the warning signal. When the animal first learns the response-consequence setup, he is understandably frightened at the prospect of being shocked. When he is shocked, he performs the response in order to escape the shock. This turns off the shock and the warning signal and the animal feels enormous relief, which becomes conditioned to the response. Later, when he learns to avoid the shock, the response is still followed by the warning signal turning off and the feeling of relief, which continues to reinforce the response.

The importance of the warning signal turning off is substantial. In one study, a standard escape/avoidance procedure was used with one important difference. When the animal performed the avoidance response, the shock was indeed avoided, but the warning signal was not. It stayed on for the usual 5 or 10 seconds whether the animal responded or not. These animal found it much

harder to learn to avoid the shock than did animals that experienced the warning signal turning off. There must be something about the

relief of *knowing* you are safe that rewards you and keeps you performing the avoidance response.

It is also critical that the shock follow the warning signal closely
in time. Usually, in laboratory preparations, the warning signal is a
tone that comes on and overlaps with the shock. Learning still
occurs, however, if the tone comes on and goes off right away,
provided the shock follows within 5 seconds or so. If the shock is
delayed by as much as 20 seconds, learning is very difficult. A tone
that comes on and goes off right away is pretty much the same as a
person shouting "Come!", so make sure that your command is
quickly followed by the shock. Because the command serves as a
warning signal in this situation, you should not continue to repeat
"come" as the dog is coming towards you. Remember, the response
should *turn off* the warning signal. Immediately switch to "good dog"
as soon as the dog turns towards you.

Here is another example of how avoidance responding works in
the real world. A dog is afraid of being in the park. In a panic, the
dog turns tail and runs home, with the owner running after him.
Even though no threat exists in the park, to the dog there is a bogey
man behind every tree. He cannot possible know there is nothing to
fear in the park because he runs away. He continues to run home
because once he escapes from the park and is on his way home, he is
flooded with relief and feels safe. Remember "Lines and Squares"
from A. A. Milne, *When We Were Very Young* (1924)?

Whenever I walk in a London street,

I'm ever so careful to watch my feet;

And I keep in the squares,

And the masses of bears,

Who wait at the corners all ready to eat

The sillies who tread on the lines of the street,

Go back to their lairs,

And I say to them, "Bears,

Just look how I'm walking in all of the squares!"As long as you stay in the squares, those bears will be kept at bay. If you never tread on the lines, how would you ever know if the bears are really there? And would it be worth the risk to find out? If the aversive stimulus is a leash jerk, it usually is worth the risk to most dogs. If it is shock, it usually isn't.

You can facilitate your dog's learning of an avoidance response by taking your time with training. Long intervals between trials leads to more efficient learning. This makes sense if the avoidance response is rewarded through feelings of relief or safety - the longer the period of time before another possible shock, the better. When I am training a recall with the electronic collar, I set my stopwatch and I make sure the interval is at least 15 minutes between trials.

### Extinction of Avoidance Responding

The persistence of avoidance responding is unmatched by any other form of learning. In one study which used 13 dogs as subjects, a very severe shock was used. After the dogs avoided the shock on ten consecutive trials, they were given 200 extinction trials (no shocks would occur whether the dogs responded or not). Every one of the dogs responded on every single trial! And not only did they continue to respond, but they continued to do so *quickly*. Of the 2600 responses, only 11 did not occur within 10 seconds of the dogs hearing the warning signal! It is the case, however, that the more dramatic effects like this are observed when a severe aversive stimulus is used. In more realistic situations, with less intense aversive stimuli, avoidance responding does extinguish eventually. Occasional use of the aversive consequence is necessary to maintain the response (unless, of course, positive consequences take over to maintain the behavior, which is the procedure I use when training recalls).

Extinction of an avoidance response can be very rapid if the avoidance response is prevented. The warning signal is presented but the dog is not permitted to make the response and so he is forced to experience the warning signal when it is not followed by shock. *Response prevention*, a.k.a. flooding, involves presenting the fearful stimulus but the animal is prevented from escaping (this is also covered in a later section). This technique can sometimes work for dogs that are fearful of other dogs. I expose such dogs to calm, friendly dogs while preventing defensive aggression (the escape response) with the use of a muzzle or a head halter and long line.

## Species-Specific Defense Reactions

Another feature of avoidance responding is that learning often occurs very rapidly. This makes sense: if an animal takes too long to learn to avoid something dangerous, he probably won't live very long anyway. Learning can be established in as few as 5-10 trials. The speed at which an avoidance response is learned depends primarily on the nature of the response. For a rat, if the response involves running into a "safe" compartment, he will learn very quickly. If the response involves running on a wheel (so the environment essentially stays the same), learning progresses more slowly. It obviously is more realistic for the rat to run and hide somewhere safe than it is to just stay in the same place.

The consideration of what is "real" for the animal brings us to the notion of *species-specific defense reactions* (SSDRs) The warning in an avoidance procedure comes to signal danger to the animal and animals have a set of behaviors that occur naturally when frightened (the "fight or flight" system). Bolles (1970) has argued that if the avoidance response you want to reinforce is one of these naturally-occurring behaviors (a SSDR), then learning will proceed rapidly. If the response is not natural for the animal in a dangerous situation, learning will progress much more slowly or not at all. These SSDRs are innately-determined, defensive behaviors; for rats, the behaviors consist of running away, crouching in one spot, defensive fighting, sticking close to walls, and seeking out dark areas. If there is an escape route, the rat will tend to flee. If there is no escape route, the rat will freeze. If a "companion" rat is placed in the same box with a rat that is being shocked, it very likely will attack the companion.

The idea of SSDRs being important in avoidance learning is supported by plenty of research. It is a breeze to teach a rat to shuttle into a compartment or to run on a wheel which opens a door to a safe area in order to avoid shock; it is nearly impossible to teach a rat to rear up on his hind legs or to press a lever to avoid shock. For this reason, it is important to analyze the response you are attempting to teach with aversive stimulation. Particularly if you are using an intense stimulus, such as shock, you should be confident that the response you are teaching is part of the dog's set of SSDRs. Recalls, go outs, and drops should be relatively easy to teach in this manner because these behaviors all resemble SSDRs (although go outs may be difficult if the dog naturally wants to run to you for safety). I have serious reservations about training other types of behaviors, such as retrieving or heeling, with shock. Furthermore, responses that are compatible with the animal's SSDRs, such as running, are learned best with an intense aversive stimulus, while responses that are less compatible with the animal's SSDRs, such as lever pressing, if learned at all, are learned best with a weak aversive stimulus.

## POSITIVE PUNISHMENT

Positive punishment consists of presenting an aversive stimulus, contingent upon a specified response. If the dog performs the response, you present the aversive stimulus. This serves to suppress the response because by not making the response, the dog is able to avoid the aversive stimulus. Remember the second half of the Law of Effect: *If a consequence is unpleasant, the preceding behavior becomes less likely.* It is not quite so simple as that, though. The negative Law of Effect implies that the punished response is gone - it has been eliminated; unlearned. But as you will see, punishment serves to *suppress* a response - but it is possible that you might see the response return at its full strength once punishment is discontinued.

Punishment has a bad rap for the same reason that escape/avoidance conditioning does: if you screw up, you can hurt your dog. However, if done right, punishment can be an extremely effective tool for eliminating behavior. The following points will aid you in the proper use of punishment when it is warranted.

## Considerations on the Use of Punishment

### How Strong Should a Punisher Be?

Generally, the more intense the aversive stimulus, the more the response will be suppressed. Low-intensity punishment produces only moderate suppression and the behavior often recovers despite continued punishment. High-intensity punishment, on the other hand, can produce complete and long-lasting suppression. Animals are able to adapt to punishment. In one study, it was found that rats trained to run down an alley for food would continue running even when severe shocks were given in the goal box, provided the rats had been exposed to a series of shocks of gradually increasing intensity. Other rats that received the intense shock from the outset stopped running completely. In other words, if you use a mild punishment initially and gradually increase the intensity, you will not see much suppression or the suppression will not last. Unfortunately, this is exactly what is typically recommended: start out with mild punishment and escalate as necessary. The dog owner uses a mild punisher at first and when that isn't effective, the level is gradually escalated over time. Each escalation produces a short-term suppression of the response and this reinforces the owner's behavior to continue with the punishment. In the end, however, there is little or no effect on the behavior because the animal is able to adapt.

A much better system is to start out with an intense punisher that does suppress the response and then use less intense punishment if the behavior reoccurs. Start off strong and then back off. This is very useful if you recommend the use of punishment to a dog owner. The owner is often more willing to use an intense punisher if she can be reassured that after the first few transgressions, the intensity of the punisher can be decreased substantially. However, the whole issue of intensity raises some pretty serious ethical questions because there is no way to know in advance how intense the initial punishment should be.

The take-home message is: Initially exposing a dog to mild punishment that does not effectively disrupt the behavior *reduces* the effect of later intense punishment. Initially exposing a dog to intense punishment that does disrupt behavior *increases* the effect of later mild punishment.

### How Important is the Immediacy of Punishment?

The delay between the response and the punisher greatly influences the degree of learning. In general, the longer the delay, the less behavior is suppressed. The "wait till your father gets home" approach to punishment is not effective.

Years ago, a study was conducted on the role of stimulus control in punishment. The study itself was very strange but it produced a pretty interesting result. The procedure went like this. A dog was permitted into a room with two bowls of dog food on the floor. The experimenter sat in between the two bowls. One bowl contained generic dog food (presumably yucky) and the other contained Alpo (presumably yummy). For dogs in Group 1, if they went to eat the Alpo, they were immediately given a resounding smack by the experimenter with a rolled-up newspaper. For dogs in Group 2, if they went to eat the Alpo, they were given a resounding smack by the experimenter with a rolled-up newspaper 5 seconds after they started eating. For dogs in Group 3, if they went to eat the Alpo, they were given a resounding smack by the experimenter with a rolled-up newspaper 15 seconds after they started eating. Soon all the dogs avoided the Alpo. Then, for the next 8 days, the experimenter no longer sat in the room but instead, watched each dog through a one-way mirror. Each day they carried out "temptation trials" in which the dog was left in the room with the two bowls of food for 10 minutes. The dogs in Group 1 (the immediate dogs) waited 2 weeks, on average, before they finally gave in and ate the Alpo (very impressive). The dogs in Group 2 (the 5 minute dogs) waited 8 days, on average, before they gave in and ate the Alpo (pretty darn good). Get this: the dogs in Group 3 (the 15 minute dogs) waited 3 whole **minutes** before eating the Alpo again! Put this in perspective though - I can think of several dog owners that I know who would be pleasantly surprised if their dogs bothered to wait until the humans left the room before scavenging from the dinner plates!

Choosing a punisher should, in part, be dictated by the immediacy with which you can deliver the punisher. For instance, the use of a spray of water from a bottle as a punisher is often impractical because the bottle is never there when you need it and you have to go hunting for it!

### What is the Right Punishment Schedule?

It is best to use a continuous schedule of punishment (FR-1). This is because the amount of response suppression that occurs is a direct function of the frequency of punishment. In other words, the more often the response is punished, the less likely it will occur again. If the response is followed by punishment every single time the response occurs, learning is most efficient.

### Does it Matter What the Punisher is?

To borrow an old saying, "the punishment should fit the crime". In other words, it is important which punisher you use. The punisher should be informative.

> "[Sitting on tacks] encourages one in learning to do something else than sit. It is not the feeling caused by punishment, but the specific action caused by punishment that determines what will be learned. To train a dog to jump through a hoop, the effectiveness of punishment depends on where it is applied, front or rear. It is what the punishment makes the dog *do* that counts." (Guthrie, 1935, p.158).

This is not to suggest that Guthrie recommends using punishment to teach a dog to jump through a hoop (!), this is merely an example of how a punisher conveys information to the animal about its own behavior. An appropriate punishment for sticking your nose into a fire is pain to your nose; an appropriate punishment for play biting should involve the dog's mouth.

### Does Punishment Teach the Animal What it Should do?

Punishing a behavior is more likely to succeed if an alternative to the punished response is provided. The alternative should also serve the same function for the animal. For instance, a dog that is punished for jumping up when greeting people faces a conflict because it is motivated to greet the person but expects punishment if it does. You can facilitate suppression of the jumping-up behavior if you teach the dog an alternative behavior that leads to the opportunity to greet (i.e., if the dog sits, the person kneels down to greet the dog). Similarly, punishing a dog for chewing inappropriate objects is much more likely to succeed if acceptable items for chewing are made available.

## Is Punishment Subject to Stimulus Control?

The stimuli that are present when a response is punished will come to serve as discriminative stimuli for punishment. If responding is consistently punished in the presence of a particular stimulus and is never punished when the stimulus is absent, the suppressive effect of the punisher will be limited to the presence of the $S^D$. This is probably one of the most frustrating aspects of punishment. In many situations, the dog owner who administers the punishment serves as the $S^D$. In other words, the dog learns that the punishment only occurs *when the owner is present*. For instance, a dog that is punished by the owner for lying on the furniture often learns to stay off the furniture only when the owner is home. In worst cases, the dog actually comes to fear the owner because she has become an aversive stimulus.

This is the reason why "remote" punishers, such as booby traps and motion-activated alarms, are usually more effective because suppression of the behavior does not come to be controlled by the owner. Remote punishers are activated by the dog's behavior, rather than by the owner, so the dog may well experience the punishment when the owner is not around. One of my most resounding successes with Shaahiin involved setting a booby trap to punish stealing food from the counter. On the edge of the counter, I set several mouse traps, *upside-down* and covered with wax paper. Just beyond the paper, I left very enticing pieces of chicken liver. Then I left for the day. Upon my return, I discovered the traps had been sprung and the liver was sitting exactly where I had left it. I left the traps and items of food there for several days but they were not touched. It has been many years now and I brag that I can leave a plate full of food on the floor and go out for the evening and it will still be sitting there when I get home.

Sometimes, remote punishers are not strong enough. I set the same type of trap for an Irish Water Spaniel. I left the room and shortly after heard the traps spring. I ran out to find her up on the counter, happily munching on the bait. My pup, Eejit, is used to the sounds of my collection of various gadgets and nothing seems to bother him. I found him settling comfortably for a nap on my brand-new Sofa Saver the other day, with the alarm blaring in his ears!

## Punishment is Rewarding to the User

The effects of punishment can be deceptive because initially, the aversive stimulation serves to suppress *all* ongoing behavior. The animal has not yet learned which response is being punished, only that punishment is likely and so it tends to stop behaving altogether (the Velcro dog syndrome!). Unfortunately for dogs, most owners like a dog that doesn't do anything and so using punishment can actually reward the owner's behavior.

## Behavior that Persists Despite Punishment

Oddly, punishment does not always suppress behavior and in some situations, it can actually serve as a signal for positive reinforcement. This is the explanation for animals (and children) that appear to actually seek out punishment. The behavior strikes people as abnormal but not if you look at the contingencies more closely. This *self-punitive behavior* appears in situations where positive reinforcement is available only when the response is punished. A dog that is habitually ignored by his owner can develop patterns of behavior that prompt the owner to punish him, but at the same time, he is receiving the attention he craves, which serves as positive reinforcement for the behavior. It would suggest that aversive consequences are better than no consequences at all. I suspect this is the case only for very social species. Dealing with self-punitive behavior is awkward because during those times when the dog is not misbehaving, the owner is so relieved to have a moment's peace that the dog is again left alone (and thus, ignored). The misbehavior becomes the only means for obtaining attention from the owner.

A very common example of punishment serving as a signal for reinforcement is observed in every beginner-level obedience class when pet owners first start teaching the sit-stay. The sit itself is still a fairly novel behavior and so each time the dog breaks from the stay, the owner requests it to sit and reinforces the sit. Then the dog is commanded to stay again (a signal for no reinforcement for awhile). However, if the dog moves again, the owner instantly comes back to request a sit and provide more reinforcement. The act of not staying and the ensuing disapproval of the owner becomes associated with a forthcoming reward. What dog in his right mind would ever bother staying?

If the idea of punishment becoming reinforcing seems a bit far-fetched, here's another example. Back when Pavlov and his associates were first learning about classical conditioning, they tried using a variety of stimuli as the CS. In one case, they tried using a severe shock as a CS for food. They discovered that if they started out with a very weak shock and gradually increased the intensity, the dogs would come to turn around, salivate, and lick at the place where the shock was delivered. In contrast, if they tried using the severe shock on dogs that had not experienced the gradual build-up in intensity, these dogs would whine, cry, and flail about rather than eat the food. So animals can learn to take a lot of punishment if they have the opportunity to adapt to it and can learn to even like it if it is associated with positive consequences.

**Vicious-cycle behavior** describes a situation in which the animal continues to perform a previously established escape response, despite the fact that the response is now punished. I tend to bite my fingernails when I am stressed. I get stressed if I am prevented from biting my fingernails (usually through the use of a bad-tasting substance which punishes my biting). Often, I find that my fingernail biting is worse after I have put the bad-tasting substance on my nails than before. I continue to bite my nails even though biting is punished because biting my nails is associated with a reduction in my feelings of stress. Performing the response is associated with a reduction of anxiety or fear and this more than compensates for the punishment.

Phobic behavior in dogs often ends up in a vicious cycle because the owner resolves to punish the defensive (avoidance) response. For instance, a dog that fears bicycles will attempt to flee or hide in the presence of a bicycle. If the owner then punishes the fearful behaviors, it is highly likely that the fearful behaviors will escalate. The dog will continue to respond fearfully, even in the face of extreme punishment, because the reduction in fear associated with avoiding bicycles is so reinforcing to the dog that it overrides the effect of the punishment.

A somewhat less extreme example is the dog that has been punished for licking faces. Licking is an appeasement gesture which serves to reduce fear in the submissive dog (because the behavior reduces the likelihood of aggression from other dogs). Punishing a dog for licking typically has the effect of increasing the likelihood of the licking response rather than suppressing it because the threat of punishment actually increases the rewarding effects of the fear reduction associated with the licking response.

### What's the Scoop on Using Punishment?

Punishment can be an extremely effective method of teaching but only if certain conditions are met. Meeting these conditions is often impossible or is so challenging that it is easier to take a different approach. First and foremost, punishment must not be used as retribution. Punishment is a learning tool, not a means for revenge. That's why Ted Turner's classification of death as punishment is incorrect: dead things don't learn.

Punishment must be initially severe, must fit the crime, must be consistent, immediate, and not reliably associated with inconvenient $S^D$s, such as a particular person. Ideally, an appropriate

alternative behavior is available. My all-time favorite example of the perfect punishment comes from Karen Pryor, in her book *Don't Shoot the Dog!*. She imagines what the world would be like if every time someone parked a car illegally, the car exploded. I suspect no one would ever park illegally! This punishment completely fits the bill: it is intense, it is immediate, it happens every time, it happens re- motely, and it fits the crime because your car no longer exists. Contrast this with the way things usually happen: I receive a ticket that doesn't have to be paid for a week or two, the fine is not heavy ($20 in Toronto), more often than not, I get away with it (I would guess I am on a FR-20 to FR-30 schedule of punishment), and if I watch for the parking enforcement officer coming down the street, I move my car and avoid a ticket. It's not a totally stupid system, though - towing _is_ an effective punisher - I have **never** parked in a tow-away zone since the first and only time I came back to find my car gone :-(!

## NONCONTINGENT AVERSIVE STIMULI

By noncontingent aversive stimuli, I mean unpleasant events that occur which are unrelated to the animal's behavior. Why is this important? Because the average dog owner doesn't know how to teach a dog effectively. Even though the owner may think she is punishing a specific behavior, to the dog the aversive events may appear to be occurring randomly and without respect to his behavior. A good example of this is the owner that punishes the dog for house soiling several hours after the misdeed took place. There is no evidence that animals are capable of associating the punishment with their previous behavior and so, as far as the dog is concerned, the punishment is not contingent upon anything he has done.

The effect of noncontingent aversive stimulation was studied in the laboratory years ago, before there were restrictions on what can and can't be done with animals. Fortunately, this type of research could no longer be conducted but it did provide useful information at the time. Martin Seligman and his associates conducted studies in which a dog was placed in a shuttle box but a barrier was in place so the dog could not shuttle back and forth between the compart- ments. He was stuck on one side. Then the dog was exposed to random shocks from which he could not escape. The shocks were delivered regardless of what the dog was doing. Initially the dog would scream, try to escape, and flail about. After a time, though, the dog would become listless, immobile, and would simply lie on the floor and take the shock. This is called *learned helplessness*. The dog has learned that the shock will happen regardless of what he does and so he becomes totally helpless and depressed. In fact, some theorists have argued that this may be the cause of depression in humans: a perceived helplessness because what the person does seems to have no effect on what happens.

What is even more interesting is that if the barrier to the safe compartment is now removed, so the dog can escape the shock, he doesn't do it. He just continues to lie there and take it. It is as though learned helplessness causes the animal to no longer monitor his own behavior and so he can't make connections between what he does and the consequences. The helpless dog can eventually learn to escape the shock but only if the experimenter goes in and physically pushes the dog back and forth across the barrier during each shock. Learning still proceeds very slowly.

I maintain that poorly socialized dogs who have spent their lives in a kennel often suffer from learned helplessness. I have seen several dogs, purchased from large-scale breeders as adults, that are unsuitable as pets because they are listless and unresponsive. It is as though they have learned that events happen, irrespective of their behavior, and they have no control. They are suffering from a generalized case of learned helplessness.

# Negative Punishment

The process of negative punishment is left until the end, not because it is ineffective or impractical but because it is relatively simple and limited in usefulness. Negative punishment refers to the procedure of taking something positive away, contingent upon an undesired behavior. By taking something positive away, you are making the probability of that undesired behavior less likely in the future, thereby punishing it.

Negative punishment can take the form of removing a reward that the dog is able to see or even taste, contingent upon some behavior you wish to eliminate. For instance, you might show the dog a treat, request a behavior, and if the dog chooses to perform an incorrect behavior (or no behavior, which is also an incorrect response), you could eat the treat yourself (or remove it from his view, if you don't relish the taste of boiled chicken liver!).

Time out is another popular application of negative punishment. Time out involves removing the animal from a source of reinforcement for a specified period of time. When a child is timed out, she normally has to go stand or sit in a corner for a few minutes while the rest of the group continues to have fun. Hockey players are timed out on the bench for undesirable behavior (with an associated increase in the likelihood that a positive punishment will also be applied in the form of a goal scored by the opposing side). Criminals are timed out by being sent to jail. When a dog is timed out, he is often placed in his crate or some other location of confinement.

I often recommend time out as a procedure for modifying play behaviors in puppies, with a slight modification. If the puppy gets too rough in his play, the owner is to abruptly time himself out, away from the puppy for a short time. The owner immediately stands up and marches out of the room, shutting the door in puppy's face. I find this more effective than removing the puppy because the puppy gets a lot of attention on the way to the crate (it may not be positive attention from the owner's perspective but it often is from the puppy's!). I also recommend a fairly short time out period because research has shown that, at least with children, a 10-minute time out can actually be detrimental as compared to a 3-minute time out. That's because the longer you leave the child, the more likely he will learn to amuse himself while alone. You don't want him learning to like being by himself. I suspect puppies would also learn lots of self-sufficient behaviors if left alone for any time. I often go with 20-30 seconds. Notice that this time out procedure is essentially what you are doing if you implement a procedure of ignoring your dog for incorrect responses to an $S^D$ (refer to the section on stimulus control and the section on conditioned reinforcers - incorrect responses can be followed by either an aversive stimulus or by no consequence, which signals to the animal that reinforcement is not forthcoming). A time out for an incorrect response to a command might be as quick as turning your back on the dog for 2-3 seconds. This often works well for a dog that is barking while responding (presumably out of frustration because he is not yet under good stimulus control or in some cases, out of excitement).

More and more agility handlers seem to be retiring from the ring after the dog makes an error, with the hope that by removing the dog from the source of reinforcement (the opportunity to perform agility obstacles), he will tend not to repeat the misbehavior (such as missing contact zones, flattening out over jumps, or not taking appropriate directions from the handler). This might well work if performed consistently but bear in mind that the dog must be cognizant of the fact that he would have been able to perform more obstacles had he not responded the way he did. The problem is that we all walk out of the agility ring at some point - does that mean we are all punishing our dog's final response on the course? Can we be sure that the dog understands when he finished the course legitimately versus when he was prevented from finishing the course? In competition, at least, you must never appear angry or upset with your dog, in the event it might appear as poor sportsmanship to the spectators and besides, most agility trainers feel that primarily positive techniques must be used to maintain the dog's attitude in agility. I am not convinced that this application of negative punishment is effective for our furry friends.

# The Application of Learning Principles to Changing Behavior

## (A.K.A. Behavior Modification Techniques)

Behavior modification involves the application of learning principles to change behavior. There are certain techniques that have been developed primarily for application, although these procedures had their start in the laboratory. Behavior modification terms are finding their way into the vocabulary of dog trainers so it is important to know their meaning and application.

### Teaching New Behaviors

When we decide to teach a dog a response, the first thing to consider is whether the response is part of the dog's behavioral repertoire. Does the dog already perform the response over which we want to gain control? For instance, if we want to teach a dog to sit on command, we are trying to obtain control over a behavior that the dog already performs. When we teach a dog to finish, we are trying to establish a new behavior that the dog has never before performed or performs with a low probability. For behaviors that are already performed, there are four potential techniques for gaining control over the response: **1** the trainer can simply wait until the behavior is performed and immediately reinforce the dog - the behavior will come to occur with greater and greater frequency (the "catch them doing it right" philosophy), **2** the trainer can "shape" the behavior by reinforcing the dog for performing successive approximations (steps), **3** the trainer can "prompt" the behavior to occur and then reinforce the dog, or **4** the trainer can use a combination of shaping and prompting. For novel behaviors, the first technique of waiting for the behavior to occur is not appropriate, for obvious reasons! The latter three techniques can be used. Let's look at what is meant by shaping and prompting.

### Shaping by Successive Approximations

Shaping by successive approximations involves a process of differentially rewarding some behaviors and not others. When you shape a dog to perform a particular behavior, you are following a procedure that leads the dog to progress by small steps. You accept as your first criterion for reinforcement some behavior that is less than the behavior you want to teach (the terminal behavior or goal response) but that somehow resembles it. For instance, if your goal is to teach your dog to roll over and if your dog lies down on command, that could be your first behavior. You reinforce this response until it occurs consistently. However, lying down is always variable and sometimes, your dog will flop over on his side. Then you should shift your criterion for reinforcement to the behavior of flopping over on one side. Once your dog is doing this consistently, you then shift

Shaping Roll-Over by Successive Approximations

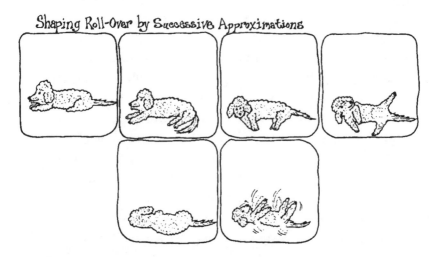

your criterion to reinforcing only those lie-downs where your dog raises his hind leg. Once he has the idea that this produces reinforcement, you shift to only reinforcing him when he lies down and rolls onto his back. You keep working in this manner until you finally achieve your goal response. Remember, you stay at one stage until the behavior is well established and then you move on.

The term "shaping by successive approximations" is widely misused in dog training circles. Shaping means that the animal's behavior is shaped or molded into a terminal response by the trainer's differential reinforcement of behavior. Successive approximations means that the trainer progresses from first accepting a response that is not the terminal response but instead approximates it. Using a shifting criterion, the animal builds upon the behavior and the trainer eventually reinforces only the terminal response. The idea of approximations seems to have permeated through to dog trainers but the notion of shaping or molding, has been missed. Many trainers use the term "shaping" as though it were synonymous with "training".

To a psychologist, shaping by successive approximations is a hands-off, non- interactive process. Imagine you are required to train a rat to press a lever whenever a light comes on. The rat is placed in a small box with only a lever, a feeder located directly underneath it, and a light placed above it. The rat is afraid of you so you cannot "show" it what to do. You wait until the rat is near the feeder and you drop food into it. Soon the rat is hanging out near the feeder. Then you decide to drop food in the feeder whenever the rat inadvertently touches the lever with a front paw. After a time, the rat is consistently touching the lever with its paw. Then you feed the rat whenever it touches the lever with sufficient force to make it move. Once this is consistently occurring, you require that the rat depress the lever all the way down before dropping food in the feeder. Through this process you have simply waited for the rat to offer behaviors and rewarded what you have defined as the desired response.

Only when the rat is reliably performing the lever-pressing response would you introduce the light. Turn the light on and reward
the next lever press. Turn the light off and refrain from rewarding the
next lever press. It is imperative to wait until the rat has acquired
the response before introducing the "command" for two reasons.
First, in the beginning, you can't be sure that the rat will perform the
response when you turn on the light. Consequently, if you introduced the light right away, you would more often than not turn the
light on and the rat would do nothing. Remember learned irrelevance or the pre-exposure effect? The rat would soon learn to
ignore the light because it is meaningless. Second, you have to
refrain from rewarding the response when the light is not on (in
order to gain stimulus control). This would mean that during the
initial acquisition stage when the rat is first learning what response
is necessary to earn reinforcement, you would sometimes not reinforce the response. This, of course, makes it extremely difficult for
the rat to learn what you want. It is far easier to wait until you have
the final behavior occurring with regularity before adding the command (if this doesn't make sense, you should re-read the section on
Stimulus Control).

Think of shaping as analogous to what often happens in real-life
learning. Through a shaping procedure, a child can learn to aim and
throw a basketball through a hoop. The child is rewarded by closer
and closer approximations as she gets closer and closer to getting
the ball into the hoop. Language acquisition is shaped in small
children. At first, mom is ecstatic with any sound that resembles an
"m". Eventually, the child discovers that something slightly longer,
"ma", results in even more excitement. Then, repeating this, "ma
ma", makes the mom go wild. Finally, the child manages to produce
something vaguely resembling "mom" and then the word becomes
cleaner and cleaner. Of course, this process might take a year or
more (I'm not up on my child development stages) but you can see
that attempts made by a baby that is just starting to make sounds is

going to be received very differently than sounds made by an older and more capable child. Maybe you remember the first time your puppy encountered a Kong stuffed with cheese whiz and kibble? Eejit started by licking the food out, which reinforced licking behavior. As the volume of cheese whiz decreased, his small puppy tongue wouldn't reach all the way in and he couldn't get to the food. As he got more and more frustrated, he moved the Kong around a bit. Eventually, a piece of kibble fell out. Wow! Gradually, licking became replaced with tossing and banging the Kong around. Occasionally a chunk fell out and Eejit's technique became refined to the point that he can empty a Kong of its contents in no time at all just by throwing it around.

Because shaping is such a hands-off technique, it is an extremely useful tool for working with fearful dogs or aggressive dogs that you cannot handle. It is also virtually the only feasible training technique for working with most wild animals that do not tolerate handling by humans.

Learning to shape requires exquisite observational skills, incredible patience, and lightening-fast decisions. You must have a mental image in your mind of what behavior you will reinforce because if you have to decide on the fly, your reinforcement will be delivered too late. You must continuously watch the animal so that no reinforcement opportunities are missed. If you try to progress through the approximations too quickly, the animal's performance will deteriorate. If you stay at one stage too long, the animal may get stuck and be unable to move onto the next stage.

One good way to get your feet wet is to play The Shaping Game. Gather a bunch of friends together and choose one to be the "dog". Everyone else decides upon a behavior to teach, such as standing on a chair or turning in a circle. A clicker is used to convey to the "dog" what behaviors you like and you work to shape the desired behavior. There can be no talking. All communication is done via the conditioned reinforcer. The hardest thing about playing this game is finding people who can behave like dogs rather than people. Most people tend to "hypothesis test". In other words, if you get them moving toward a blackboard, they suddenly begin erasing the board or grabbing a piece of chalk and marking on it. Dogs usually don't behave as though they are trying to figure you out (although some dogs who are sophisticated in the game of shaping do appear to be doing exactly that - I believe these dogs have acquired a learning set for shaping because they catch on extremely quickly to new behaviors).

Karen Pryor listed "Ten Laws of Shaping" in her *Don't Shoot the Dog!*:

**1** When you raise your criteria, do so in increments that are small enough that the animal has a chance of succeeding.

**2** Make sure you stick with one aspect of the behavior at a time: for instance, don't try to shape both the closeness and the straightness of the sit-in-front at the same time.

**3** Make sure the animal is accustomed to intermittent reinforcement for the current level of the behavior before shifting your criterion. You must be able to sustain responding in case the animal doesn't manage to attain your next approximation within the first couple of attempts.

**4** If you are asking for a new level of the behavior, relax your other expectations: when I train a young dog on weave poles, we start off with speed, then switch to accuracy, and finally try to put it all together. When I switch to accuracy, often the dog will slow down at first.

**5** Plan ahead - you must have a picture in your head of the behaviors you intend to reinforce and what the progression will look like because your animal may skip ahead at any point and you must be ready to move with him.

**6** Don't allow different people to work with the same animal on a specific behavior - it is too difficult to keep the criterion escalating consistently.

**7** If you aren't getting anywhere with one approach to shaping a behavior, try something different.

**8** Pay attention to your animal! You must not miss behaviors that should be reinforced. It is too confusing for the animal.

**9** If the animal's behavior deteriorates, "go back to kindergarten". Don't be afraid to regress occasionally. Be flexible.

**10** As with all animal training, quit while you're ahead. End on a positive note.

Marian Breland and Robert Bailey (of *Animal Behavior Enterprises*) recommend working with two very different species in order to fine-tune shaping skills. The chicken is a good example of an animal that moves very quickly and emits many behaviors in a short period of time. You really have to be on your toes to shape a chicken. The Dutch rabbit is a good choice for refining your patience and observational skills because these rabbits are fairly lethargic, move slowly, and emit few behaviors in a comparable period of time. You really have to stay awake to shape a rabbit! If you can't manage a chicken and a rabbit in your home, I recommend educational software programs which provide the opportunity to shape a rat in a Skinner box. **Sniffy the Virtual Rat** is a program of a computer-simulated rat that can be shaped to perform a few simple behaviors. **CyberRat** is a program containing video images of a rat that can be shaped to perform virtually any behavior contained in the video footage.

### Prompting

Shaping takes patience, careful observation, and good timing. It is an extremely useful technique for teaching animals that do not interact well with humans (i.e. rats and pigeons tend to become frightened when touched) or that live in a different environment (i.e.

marine mammals). For these situations, a hands-off approach is necessary.

However, many animals can be *prompted* to perform behaviors that we wish to train. Dogs are particularly good for prompting because they are accustomed to us leading them around and showing them the ropes. Prompting involves manipulating the animal or the environment such that the animal performs the response. An example of a physical prompt is pushing down on the dog's hind end to encourage a sit response. An example of a visual prompt is a lure (treat) that is moved in such a way that the dog follows it and performs the response; the treat is raised above the dog's nose and he assumes a sitting position in order to look at it. A prompt is essentially anything that encourages the animal to perform the response.

Prompting

Prompting can be more efficient than shaping for the acquisition of behavior because the behavior usually starts happening much more quickly. The problem comes when you try to get rid of the prompt. Prompts must be gradually *faded* so that the animal learns to perform the behavior without the prompt. For instance, many trainers set up two boards from the broad jump and stand in between to encourage a dog to come in straight and sit in front. How do you fade out such an obvious prompt? Once the dog is reliably coming in straight, you switch to using two smaller white boards. Provided the dog continues to come in straight, switch to shorter boards. If he still continues to reliably come in straight, switch to even smaller boards, and paint them to resemble whatever surface you are training on so the dog will find them more difficult to see. If all goes well at this stage, switch to using short dowels or pencils. Eventually, your dog will not require any prompt to still continue to some in straight. Whenever you opt for prompting over shaping, be sure that you can foresee how you will gradually fade out the prompt.

Obviously, how dependent a dog will become on a prompt varies with the type of prompt you are using. Tactile prompts seem to be particularly salient to dogs. Visual prompts are easier to fade, although many pet owners using the lure/reward method have trouble fading the treat lure. This leads to the common complaint that "my dog only does something if he knows I have food". That is because the visual prompt has not been faded out.

Not only does prompting produce faster initial results, but you can add the cue as soon as you determine that you can reliably elicit the behavior with the prompt. If you can do that, then you needn't worry about learned irrelevance. Give the command, give the prompt, reinforce the behavior. The dog will not learn any differently than if you had shaped the behavior. He still learns what behavior to perform long before he comes under good stimulus control but I would wager a guess that learning is more rapid, even if you have to go through a complicated procedure to fade the prompts.

Let me repeat a sentence from the last paragraph. "The dog will not learn any differently than if you had shaped the behavior." Some people are under the impression that shaped responses are learned "better" or retained longer than prompted responses. There is absolutely no evidence to support this view. Dogs do not learn the responses any differently. I have heard people argue that when you shape a behavior, the dog learns better because he has to "figure it out". even though it may sometimes appear so, animals do not learn by testing various possibilities. They learn by behaving in a certain way and if the behavior leads to a good state of affairs, they are more likely to do it again. That's why sometimes you think your dog has "got it" and then all of the sudden he stops responding for a time. Then the behavior comes back. That's the law of probabilities working. If he were testing different ideas, then learning would be all or none. He'd either have it or he wouldn't - the lightbulb phenomenon.

I do ackowledge that some dogs seem to understand how to play the Shaping Game. The trainer stands with a clicker and the dog starts offering all sorts of behaviors, occasionally even novel ones. As I mentioned earlier, I believe these dogs have acquired a learning set or a strategy for success in this situation. "Do stuff because eventually something will result in reinforcement." In the lab, pigeons have even been trained to offer a different behavior on each and every trial of a session. Only novel behaviors are rewarded and the birds can learn this.

So there is no "better" way, no "superior" way. Prompt when appropriate, shape when appropriate, or combine the two and prompt successive approximations to a behavior. Some dogs are distracted too much by physical prompts, some by food lures. Other dogs become very reliant on prompts and rarely offer much unsolicited behavior in a training session. Be flexible and try different techniques with each dog. They will respond differently depending upon their past learning history (also called *reinforcement history*).

## Chaining

Chaining is appropriate for teaching a complex sequence of responses. The behaviors are chained together in such a way that each behavior the animal performs is a signal for the next behavior. Reinforcement is only provided for the final behavior in the chain. With *backward chaining*, the end (terminal) behavior is established first because this response leads directly to reinforcement. Once this behavior is well established, you introduce the next-to-the-end behavior. Then you practice the two final components over and over until well established. The most recent behavior does not need to be reinforced with a primary reward because the behavior is rewarded with the opportunity to perform the end behavior, which does lead to reinforcement. For example, to teach a dog to negotiate an agility obstacle called the see-saw, the dog is initially placed on the end of the see-saw and permitted to step off (if you are concentrating on hitting contact zones, you should reward the dog before he has stepped off all the way). Once he is comfortable with this, you place him a bit further back on the plank. He steps forward and finds himself in the same position as before, and he knows he can trot off. Backwards you proceed until the dog is placed on the balance point. This is a bit more traumatic for some dogs but because he is totally comfortable with the see-saw once he balances it and can trot off, his movement forward to tip the plank is rewarded by the last part of the chain (I would lessen the tip at first and gradually introduce increasing board movement). Eventually, you have a dog that is comfortable running onto the see-saw, tipping it, and trotting off. This is an example of using backward chaining to perform a complex response.

Backward chaining can also be used to teach a dog to reliably perform a sequence of already-acquired responses. When I was trialing Shaahiin in Open, I found that he became more and more stressed as the routine progressed. I inevitably got no front on the broad jump exercise. I remedied this situation by practicing the

## Backward Chaining

broad jump over and over again, each time following it with a very special reward I did not practice the other exercises at all. Once he was doing the broad jump and reliably looking for his special reward at the end, I added in the retrieve over the high jump exercise. Each time he finished this exercise, we immediately moved over to the broad jump and completed it so he could get his special reward. Once he had this routine down, I added in the retrieve on the flat exercise. You get the picture. In the end, heeling was reinforced by the opportunity to do the figure eight exercise, which was reinforced by the opportunity to do the drop on recall, which was reinforced with the opportunity to do the retrieve on the flat, which was reinforced by the opportunity to do the retrieve over the high jump, which was reinforced by the opportunity to do the broad jump, which was reinforced with a very special reward!

Forward chaining can also be done but the results are never as nice as with backward chaining. That's because you have to start by rewarding the first behavior in the sequence and then switch to rewarding the second behavior in the sequence when it is introduced, and so on. The reward never follows a specific behavior consistently so the chain is not as well established. In order for chaining to work, the sequence of behaviors must be consistent. That's why chaining is not appropriate for teaching a dog to perform a series of agility obstacles. In competition, the obstacles are never in the same sequence. Some agility trainers do chain their dogs to always finish on the table and these dogs find it very difficult to pass by a table without jumping on it!

Sometimes a combination of forward and backward chaining is used. Chaining is what is being done whenever a trainer breaks down an exercise into its component parts and teaches each separately. Few trainers teach dogs to heel by attaching a leash and going for a walk. Most break the exercise down and teach the dog to step off on the command "heel", to sit automatically with a stop, to turn left with certain footwork, to turn right with certain footwork, to about-turn with certain footwork, to move slowly and to move fast. Once the dog has perfected each individual component, the parts can be joined to produce a flowing sequence of heeling behaviors. Some trainers mistakenly call this procedure successive approximations but this is incorrect. Successive approximations refers to a process in which you initially reinforce a behavior that is not what you really want but possesses some, potentially vague, likeness to what you really want. You gradually build on variations of that behavior to get to the final goal. With chaining, you build a group of component pieces. All are legitimate pieces of the whole but are established separately before being joined together into a chain.

It is always easier to interrupt a chain of behaviors early in the sequence than later. An example would be a dog that takes off for the flyball box when it isn't his turn. If the handler notices right away, the dog can sometimes be called back. But if the dog is already in full run over the jumps, good luck! This also works for dogs that perform their own "untrained" sequences of behavior. As a youngster, Eejit was terrible for running up to people and jumping on them. I didn't want to punish him for his sociable behavior because I wanted a friendly dog. So I set out to call him to me for a treat whenever I thought he might want to run up to someone. If I caught him early, just when he spied the person, I could get him to come. If I waited a split second too long and called him after he had already started to run, he wouldn't come. That's because the reward from jumping up was too close and I couldn't compete with my measly little treat. Once he caught on to the idea that walking towards people meant getting treats from me, then I was able to successfully call him later and later in the sequence. Now I can usually interrupt the sequence anywhere, even in mid-leap.

With dogs that are aggressive toward strangers, this notion of interrupting the sequence is also useful. Often, the dog can be distracted with treats if you manage to interrupt the sequence early. While the person is still a long way off, bring out the treats and get the dog focused on you, rather than the person coming towards you. If you are successful in distracting the dog early enough, you can sometimes cause him to not notice the person at all as you pass. However, if you wait until the dog is lunging and growling before trying to get his attention, no amount of treats will get through to him. The reward of human flesh is too close!

## Autoshaping

One of the most interesting discoveries in the area of learning theory is *autoshaping*. Let me begin with an explanation. Pigeons are typically trained to peck a lit key in a Skinner box through shaping by successive approximations (á la operant conditioning). Training a pigeon to peck a key is incredibly easy; almost too easy. That's because classical conditioning plays a major role in this training. The procedure works like this. When you first start training a pigeon to peck a key, you simply arrange to have the key light up, followed by the delivery of food. The pigeon doesn't have to do anything. It learns that the key lights up (the CS), which is a signal that food will be delivered momentarily (the UCS). Initially the pigeon approaches the feeder and pecks around it, waiting for the food. However, after a few pairings like this, the pigeon starts to approach the *key* and peck around it, waiting for the food. This pecking of the key is a conditioned reinforcer because the pigeon is not <u>required</u> to peck at the key. Of course, the experimenter then reinforces this pecking, which serves to increase the likelihood that the pigeon will peck there again and we're off to the races. In fact, shaping is not necessary at all - if the procedure is set up so that the bird learns to anticipate food when the key lights up, the bird will inevitably begin directing food-related behaviors toward the key itself. This happens despite the fact that the food will be delivered regardless of what the bird does. The important point is that the pigeon is not required to peck in order to get food - the bird does it anyway. This is autoshaping. This is magazine training taken one step further.

The autoshaped response is so strong that the animal will continue to respond *even if making the response means that food will not be delivered*. In other words, you can set up a procedure in which a lit key signals the delivery of food, *unless* the bird pecks at the key. If the bird pecks, then no food. That poor bird will continue to peck because pecking is a CR elicited by the CS (the lit key). When arranged to conflict, the classically conditioned behavior wins out over the operant contingency of "don't peck and you'll get food". Remember the section on the Brelands' "misbehaviors"? That was the same phenomenon - the animal couldn't help but direct food-related behaviors at the signal for food, even though it meant that the food wasn't delivered because of those behaviors.

In another tortuous experiment, pigeons were placed in a long alley, with the key at one end and the feeder at the other. Once the birds had learned the association between the lit key and the food delivery, they couldn't help but run down the alley to the key when it lit up, even though this meant that they didn't have time to run to the other end, where the feeder was, to get the food before it disappeared!

Dogs, as well, tend to approach a stimulus which signals food. In one study, dogs were placed in a room with two keys, one on either wall. One key (the CS+) signaled the delivery of food, the other key (the CS-) signaled that no food would be forthcoming. After learning these associations, the dogs tended to avoid the CS- when it lit up but when the CS+ lit up, the dogs would go to the vicinity of the CS+ before moving on to where the feeder was located. Some dogs would even paw at the key, nuzzle it, lick it, and/or bark at it. For those of you who have used a clicker as a conditioned reinforcer, I'm sure you recognize this list of behaviors. I have lost a few clickers by forgetting to put it out of reach, only to discover that Eejit has tried to "eat" it!

Autoshaping is an excellent starting procedure for trainers wishing to teach retrieving in a positive fashion. I was once presented with a Soft-Coated Wheaten Terrier that refused to voluntarily pick anything up in his mouth at all - even tennis balls soaked in liver juice! For fun, I decided to autoshape/shape Morgan to take the dumbbell in his mouth. Until the stage where I presented the dumbbell to Morgan to take, I never even touched him. Morgan, who was hungry because I had him skip a meal, was put into an exercise pen twice a day. Every now and then (on average every 75 seconds), I lowered a dumbbell into the pen and then dropped a piece of food into the bowl. After awhile Morgan started watching the dumbbell, waiting for it to move. It took approximately 200 pairings like this, but eventually Morgan began nosing and licking at the dumbbell. Up to this point, Morgan didn't have to do anything to obtain the food. The food was delivered regardless of whether he reacted to the dumbbell or not. Once he was reliably reacting to the dumbbell, I switched to actively shaping Morgan (I switched to operant conditioning). Then he was required to do something in order to be reinforced. At first, whenever he nosed the dumbbell, I dropped a piece of food into the bowl. Then I required that he lick it before dropping the food. Next, I required that he open his mouth next to the dumbbell. Then, he had to open his mouth over the dumbbell. Then he had to open his mouth over the middle of the dumbbell. Finally he had to actually hold the dumbbell in his mouth momentarily before receiving food. When he did this reliably 70-80 times, I sat in the pen with Morgan and presented the dumbbell in my hand for him to take. No problem - he grabbed it! Before sending Morgan back to his owner, I made sure he would take the dumbbell from my hand in a variety of settings. The whole procedure took only 3 days, two sessions per day.

## Modifying Existing Behaviors

### Conditioned Emotional Responses

The Story of Little Albert

Back in 1920 (before there were regulations against these kinds of procedures), Watson and Raynor showed that phobias could be established via classical conditioning procedures. Albert was an 11-month-old child who initially showed no fear of a white rat. However, in the experiment, every time Albert was shown the rat, a very loud noise was sounded. The loud noise caused Albert to startle and

Little Albert

show fear. In this setup, the rat is the CS and the noise is the UCS. After a few pairings, the rat alone began to elicit conditioned fear responses from Albert. He would cry and try to crawl away from the rat. In fact, Albert did the same thing when shown a dog, a rabbit, a fur coat, and a package of cotton wool! None of these things elicited fear from Albert prior to the experiment. This is an example of a *conditioned emotional response* (CER). Many fearful responses in dogs are established in this manner. CERs are extremely powerful and very resistant to extinction.

## Counterconditioning and Desensitization

If a CS has come to signal a pleasant UCS ("good dog"), it is extremely difficult to switch the CS to signal an aversive UCS ("good dog"→ a spanking). Try making the sound of kibble dropping into your dog's bowl a signal for a scolding. You'd have a very hard time of it. It is also very difficult to take a CS that has been associated with something unpleasant (the sound of a scolding voice) and make it a signal for something good. Unfortunately, this is the task of anyone who attempts to *countercondition* and *desensitize*. Counterconditioning and desensitization are useful techniques for eliminating CERs, particularly fearful behavior. The counterconditioning process involves taking a fear-provoking stimulus (the CS) which has come to be associated with an unpleasant situation and changing the association to one of signaling a pleasant situation. For instance, dogs that are fearful of strangers coming into the home are conditioned to associate the arrival of people with the delivery of food (pizza delivery people are perfect - only remember, the dog must get the pizza!).

Because switching a CS from unpleasant to pleasant can be very difficult, desensitization is also often incorporated to enhance the reversal. Desensitization involves presenting low levels of the fear-provoking stimulus and gradually working up to the full-blown stimulus. So, if your dog is fearful of strangers at the door, the first step would be to associate the presence of a stranger standing on the sidewalk with food. Once the dog is able to relax and eat while someone stands on the sidewalk, the distance the person stands from the front door is gradually reduced. Eventually, the dog is able to handle having someone standing on the front step. The next step would be having the person open the front door while the dog is being fed. The process continues until the dog is relaxed and looking forward to people coming in the house because this has come to be associated with food. This type of procedure can be lengthy, spending several days or even weeks at each stage.

Counterconditioning is the idea behind William Campbell's "jollying" procedure. If your dog is bothered by certain sounds or sights, you can act like a fool and convince the dog to relax and play in the context of these stimuli. Ciaran was quite frightened of children when he was young and the first time I entered him in an obedience match, I realized I had a problem because he was so distracted by the presence of children around the ring that he couldn't focus on what I was asking him to do. I spent the next year or so going into the "jolly" routine whenever we saw children. I'd sound really excited and then I'd whip out the Frisbee and convince him to play. At first, he could only manage to play if the kids were a fair distance away but gradually he became more tolerant. Finally, I was able to have kids throw the Frisbee for him. He always brought it back to me and I would hand it to one of the kids. The final step was having Ciaran give the Frisbee to a kid to throw. Now I don't need to worry about whether there will be children around the ring when I show. To Ciaran, children are Frisbee-throwers - they used to be scary but now they have become associated with something Ciaran enjoys very much.

Alternatively, a CS that signals a pleasant UCS can be introduced simultaneously with the CS that elicits fear. Eli Barlia (1988) describes a procedure in which he first taught a dog to associate a pair of gloves (the CS) with a number of pleasant UCSs (food, play, cuddles, etc.). Once the association was firmly established, he combined the pleasant CS (the gloves) with the fear-eliciting CS (strangers). He found that initially the dog became very tense and concerned when approached by the stranger but once the hand with the glove was extended, the dog's expression changed to one of relaxation and the dog allowed the stranger to pet him. The presentation of the pleasant CS served to weaken the conditioned response to the aversive CS. Bear in mind that this was not the only technique that was involved. The dog had also received extensive training to the point that he could be controlled in the presence of strangers - however, before the introduction of the pleasant CS (the gloves) his body and facial expression indicated that he was still nervous and tense. With the gloves, the dog was eventually able to interact and play with new people, even after they took the gloves off.

## Flooding/ Response Prevention

A form of therapeutic treatment known as *flooding* or *response prevention* is actually an extinction procedure, in which the CS is presented without the UCS. Imagine a person has acquired a deathly fear of snakes (a conditioned emotional response). Flooding would involve putting the person in a room full of snakes (friendly ones, of course), sometimes even covering the person with snakes. Because the snakes are not dangerous, the presence of the snakes (the CS) is experienced without the perceived danger (the UCS). Sometimes, this form of treatment works and the fear extinguishes. More often than not, however, the person experiences such fright and discomfort during the experience that the fear becomes even stronger. This is because the fearful emotion is usually accompanied by responses that serve to decrease the fear (i.e. escape and avoidance behaviors) and these responses are very resistant to extinction. Try forcing a dog that is fearful of people on roller-blades to sit next to a sidewalk as person after person goes by on roller-blades. The dog will become extremely jumpy and will continually try to escape. When the escape is thwarted, this too is extremely frightening and so the fear escalates to new heights. The only way that flooding will work in such a situation is to wait until the dog has become exhausted and is physically unable to respond fearfully any longer. At this point, it is actually experiencing the feared stimulus without reacting and extinction is able to occur. Usually, this is not ethical option.

Another way to extinguish a fear response is to identify a stimulus that elicits a behavior that is incompatible with fear and to present that stimulus in conjunction with the feared stimulus (very much like Barlia's procedure except using UCSs rather than CSs). Often a dog that fears people is fine if the people are accompanied by dogs. The presence of other dogs elicits behaviors that are incompatible with fear, such as play and social affiliation. In this context, the dog may barely notice approach, petting, and even hugging to the extent that the dog's fear completely extinguishes. Then, before attempting to introduce the dog to people on their own, the dog is exposed to the same, familiar people that he has learned to accept, without their dogs. This will enhance the likelihood of generalization to novel people without dogs.

### Taste Aversion Learning

The study done by Garcia and Koelling which I described earlier (in the section on Stimulus Control) demonstrates _taste aversion learning_. Animals are very quick to learn if a particular food has made them ill. In fact, they can learn the association with only one experience and they do this even though there is a long delay between eating the food and becoming ill. This makes good adaptive sense. If you become ill from something, you don't want to turn around and eat it again. In fact, wild rats are very hesitant if they encounter a new food. They eat only a small amount and then wait several hours before trying it again. That's why it's so hard to poison rats.

Animals tend to associate an illness with a novel food over a familiar food. If your dog gets into the garbage and eats a chocolate bar and some left-over kibble and then he becomes ill, he'll likely attribute the illness to the chocolate bar and not to the very familiar kibble he eats everyday. Humans are the same way. How many people do you know who swear never to touch Chinese (or Japanese or Mexican or Cuban or whatever) because they were ill after trying this type of food for the first time? They can't even bear to try it again.

Another neat thing about taste aversion learning is that the animal learns to avoid the particular type of food in all situations. This is very different to other forms of classical conditioning. For instance, if you use a sound to signal shock, the animal will come to tremble and flinch when it hears the sound, but only in the context in which the shock occurred. If the animal heard the same sound while walking down the street, it wouldn't show a conditioned response. Taste aversion learning is different though - the animal shows revulsion whenever and where ever it encounters the food.

Several years ago there was a concerted effort made to establish taste aversions in coyotes and wolves for the taste of sheep. Sheep carcasses which were laced with lithium chloride were scattered about. In some cases, this procedure worked. In one film, two wolves were placed in a pen with a sheep. The wolves had undergone lithium chloride poisonings and the animals were totally unsure what to do. After first trying to chase the sheep and discovering they disliked the taste of the wool, they tried to engage the sheep in play. They also displayed a lot of displacement behaviors (these are behaviors that seem totally unrelated to the situation at hand but are the result of conflicting motivations like wanting to prey on the sheep but being repulsed by it), such as snapping at grass, grooming, scratching, and yawning. However, other predators were unable to make the association because they had so much previous experience eating sheep. And some made the association between the *taste* of sheep and the illness but still continued to kill sheep, they just wouldn't eat them!

In a study conducted by Carl Gustavson, Ph.D., a number of different conditioning procedures were used to discourage rats from eating highly desirable Oreo® cookies. The procedures included electric shock for eating the cookie (a treatment procedure that is sometimes used to treat dogs with coprophagy), placing an unpleasant taste (quinine) in the rat's mouth while eating the cookie, shoving ammonia in the rat's face while eating the cookie, and taste aversion conditioning using lithium chloride. Only the taste aversion conditioning was effective in totally eliminating the rats' desire to eat Oreo® cookies. In the other conditions, the rats acted afraid of the cookie but would gradually approach it and tentatively begin touching it and finally, would eat it.

Dr. Gustavson tried to establish taste aversion learning in a number of dogs that eat stool (coprophagy). Instead of injecting the animal with lithium chloride, the stools are laced with it. He experienced considerable success with this technique. It is important to use just the right amount of lithium chloride because if you use too little, the dog does not ingest enough to become ill, and if you use too much, the dog will simply learn to avoid salty-tasting stools. It is a tricky (and messy!) procedure but it can be extremely effective. We do not as yet fully understand the best way to establish taste aversion conditioning in dogs suffering from coprophagy and unfortunately, Dr. Gustavson died before he was able to really establish a representative collection of case results. His wife and son continue to operate Bio-Behavioral Technology, Inc. and coprophagy kits can be purchased by calling 602-897-1541 or writing 243 W. Calle Monte Vista, Tempe, AR 85284.

## Some Common Behavior Problems

The difficulty with incorporating this section is that I don't want to even suggest that a cookbook approach to treating behavior problems is appropriate. Rarely are situations easy and straightforward. Analyzing and treating a behavior problem and arriving at an accurate diagnosis is a complex procedure that demands excellent observation and interviewing skills and the ability to generate and test likely hypotheses. Then it is necessary to design an intervention procedure that is above all, safe, and is relatively easy and practical to implement and that is highly likely to be successful. There is a need for flexibility and creativity in the event that Plan A does not work (which happens more often than not). Finally, a successful behavioral intervention requires frequent assessments over a fairly long time frame to ensure the problem does not recur.

Having said that, I will discuss a few common behavior problems and some of the obvious forms of intervention, all of which have been discussed within this book.

### Phobias

Dogs occasionally suffer from phobias. I have seen various noise phobias, movement phobias (such as hand shyness), floor phobias, people phobias, and even a black rabbit phobia! Thunder is one of the most common noise phobias. In most cases, phobias can be analyzed in terms of conditioned emotional responses. The fear-eliciting stimulus is the CS and the reaction felt by the animal is the UCS. There are exceptions though. There is some indication that fear of thunder may have a genetic basis (which would make thunder a UCS). And certainly neophobia (fear of novel things) is a characteristic adult behavior of most any wild species (I'm sure this is why most people start out voting liberal and, as they age, end up voting conservative!).

If phobias are conditioned emotional responses, then it is necessary to somehow disrupt the association made by the animal between the fear it feels and the stimulus it perceives. This can be done through:

**1** habituation.

**2** desensitization and counterconditioning.

**3** flooding.

Usually a combination of techniques is most effective.

To alleviate a dog's fear of thunder, as an example, the usual approach is to determine a way to simulate the feared stimulus, usually by means of a recording of a thunderstorm. If this is not sufficient (the dog is under control of more than just the auditory component of storms), then it may be necessary to use strobe lights to simulate lightening, running the shower (even with cookie pans in the tub) to simulate the sound of rain on the rooftop, and some behaviorists have even tried using negative ion generators (with relatively little

**Desensitization & Counterconditioning**

success) to simulate what happens in the air just prior to a storm. Once you have a means for presenting the feared stimulus, you conduct sessions in which the dog is repeatedly exposed to extremely low levels of the stimulus (habituation). After many trials, the volume is ever-so-slightly increased (systematic desensitization). All the while, the dog is being encouraged to relax and enjoy himself while the session is going on (counterconditioning). The owner might be feeding the dog or rubbing the dog's tummy and massaging his muscles. Some behaviorists incorporate the use of an additional olfactory cue (a distinctive smell such as an air freshener) that is only present when the sessions are being conducted. The dog learns that this stimulus signals that all is well - this is just a fake storm. Gradually, over many, many long sessions (remember, long sessions enhance long-term habituation), the volume is up to the max and the dog is still zoning out, cool as a cucumber. At this point, it is appropriate to begin fading out the olfactory cue so that hopefully, the dog will be unable to discriminate between fake storms and the real thing. It is critical that during the treatment proceedings, the dog never, ever be exposed to the feared stimulus at full intensity. Otherwise, you reinstitute the conditioned fear. Consequently, it is only feasible to work on thunder phobia in the off-season.

Other phobias are less suited to such a clean desensitization and counterconditioning procedure. Fear of strangers or other dogs is more difficult because you can only decrease the level of the stimulus by presenting it at a distance. Sometimes, this is not sufficient to simulate the real thing. In such situations, counterconditioning may be the best bet. Each time a scary dog walks past, the dinner bowl is pulled out of hiding. Or flooding may be the procedure of choice. Introduce the dog to numerous friendly, low-key, submissive dogs and gradually build him up to be able to stand the hyperactive, playful pups and assertive adults. This is a combination of desensitization and flooding.

With any phobia, you must guard against sensitization. Always monitor the dog's behavior to ensure his reactions are not worsening. Some fearful dogs can only handle very short sessions, such as quick walks to give them minimal but necessary exposure to the world. They need to get out to be exposed to stimuli but if they reach a point of overload, they become sensitized and begin reacting to every little thing.

### Separation Anxiety

Separation anxiety is also a phobia but it warrants special consideration. Some dogs seem to be extremely socially affiliative and find it very difficult to be alone. Others have had frightening experiences while alone and have come to associate the experience with the owner's absence. I even had one case where, after a rash of mid-afternoon thunderstorms (the UCS), the dog came to associate being left alone (the CS) with the advent of a storm.

Along the same lines as described above, the most successful form of treatment is one in which the dog is gradually exposed to the feared stimulus (being left alone), while at the same time, associating that stimulus with a pleasant, relaxing event such as eating. The difficult part is that often there is no minimal amount of being left alone that the dog can handle. It begins to display fear the moment the owner even thinks about leaving. The first task is then to teach the dog the irrelevance of the leaving cues. The owner must engage in leaving behaviors but not leave, mix up the order of the cues, and generally induce a state of confusion in the dog so he never knows if you're coming or going! Then the goal is to teach the dog to handle being able to sit on the opposite side of the door from the owner. The owner first works on the sit-stay, then the sit-stay while the owner opens and steps behind a door in the house (such as the bathroom). Immediately, the owner pops back out and rewards the dog for staying. Gradually, the time the owner spends on the other side of the door increases. Then, the dog learns to perform the same exercise at various doors, including the front door. When the dog is

able to sit-stay for as long as 1-2 minutes, the owner introduces a
safety cue that tells the dog these are just fake departures and the
owner is really just on the other side of the door. Some dogs come
equipped with an already established safety cue, such as a bag of
rubbish. Otherwise, I often use a Kong stuffed with cheese whiz,
which the dog may or may not touch while left alone. The cue is
removed immediately when the owner returns. The dog is gradually
left for longer and longer periods of time, although he is likely to lie
down rather than sit on the other side of the door. Once he is able to
wait for several hours, the safety cue is faded out and the owner can
go off to work without the dog ever realizing that he is not just
around the corner, waiting to pop in at any moment.

A dog suffering from separation anxiety must never be left alone
except during the planned absences. Like any other fear, exposure to
the full-blown association of the stimulus and the fear will interfere
with attempts to desensitize and countercondition.

### Interdog Aggression

Dogs behave aggressively toward other dogs for a variety of
reasons. Sometimes it is the result of fluctuating hormones, sometimes the dog has been poorly socialized and has no idea that dogs
are sociable creatures, sometimes the dog has been attacked or
frightened by a dog and has generalized the experience to a group of
dogs or to all dogs, sometimes the dog feels trapped and vulnerable
on a leash and cannot approach other dogs calmly, sometimes the
dog has been reinforced by the owner for behaving aggressively
toward other dogs, sometimes the aggression is the result of displacement behavior or frustration because he is never permitted to
socialize, sometimes the dog is extremely sensitive to being touched
by other dogs, or any combination of these! This list could probably
go on and on. That's why it is so critical to be a good listener and to
ask good questions. More than anything, you have to be a good
observer because the dog's body postures and behaviors will usually

provide a wealth of information (so will the reactions of the other dogs).

The treatment of interdog aggression demands flexibility. Sometimes response prevention and flooding work, if you can expose the dog to other dogs safely. Sometimes counterconditioning works. You teach the dog to expect food or play which is signaled by the presence of other dogs. Sometimes you can actually shape affiliative behaviors. I use a clicker to mark and reinforce behaviors such as approaching and sniffing another dog. This also serves to interrupt the interaction before it switches from positive to negative. Gradually, the owner demands more sustained positive interactions before reinforcing the dog. Sometimes, it is necessary to punish aggressive behaviors so that the dog begins to inhibit the aggression, which then provides the owner with an opportunity to incorporate more positive procedures. Sometimes, simply introducing a fearful dog to new dogs from behind (without a face-on approach) is all that is necessary to eliminate the aggression. Afterwards, these same dogs, who are now acceptable, can be met face-on. Sometimes removing the leash and allowing the dog to interact with other dogs freely will eliminate the aggressive behaviors. This is one problem for which there is definitely no easy answer.

### Aggression Toward People

Aggression toward people can be subdivided into two types: aggression toward family members and aggression toward strangers. Aggression toward strangers is usually fear-motivated or territorial. Territorial aggression is the easier of the two with which to deal. Desensitization and counterconditioning are most effective. People approach the area but do not come close enough to elicit a full-blown response. The owner engages in feeding or playing with the dog to countercondition a different response in reaction to the stimulus of an approaching person. Countercommanding may also be helpful. Over time, the people move closer and closer to the area until the dog is able to tolerate direct approaches into the yard or home.

Fear-motivated aggression is a bit trickier because it is often more difficult to engage the dog in an alternative behavior. Countercommanding is also a useful adjunct to use in combination with desensitization and counterconditioning or as a backup procedure. When dealing with Ciaran's fear of children, I taught him to "go away" which meant move away from where you are. Then, when I saw him beginning to look uncomfortable, I requested that he "go away", which was a form of countercommanding. The nice thing about this is that now he often initiates the response himself without being told. This is ideal - a dog that recognizes he is feeling uncomfortable and moves away rather than trying to frighten off the scary thing.

I have encountered a couple of dogs that show predatory aggression toward small children. You can determine this in part by observing how they react around still, quiet children versus moving, squeaky children. If it is the movement or the noise that triggers the response, it very likely is predatory. Sometimes, a strong punisher is the most expedient means for eliminating predatory aggression.

Likewise, dogs that show aggression or chase behavior in response to people jogging by, people on roller blades and bicycles, and even cars are very likely exhibiting predatory aggression. Desensitization and counterconditioning can sometimes work for these problems. The other alternative is punishment. Remember, though, if punishment is going to be effective, it must be intense, timed precisely, and should work in only a few trials. In these cases, I never pair a warning with the delivery if the aversive stimulus. The point is for the dog to associate the delivery of the punisher with the stimulus, not with the trainer.

Aggression toward family members is a whole different kettle of fish. Often, it appears to be defensive aggression ("you're not going to get to punish me this time!"). Possessive aggression is also common. This is a behavior pattern that is reasonably normal within dogs, with some dogs showing more possessive tendencies than others. Puppies can easily be taught that humans are no threat to their possessions and so they have no reason to behave aggressively. If the dog is already an adult, it is much more difficult to accomplish this teaching. Again, a desensitization and counterconditioning procedure often works. Also, the context is changed as radically as possible. The dog is fed from a hand rather than a bowl, in a different room, at a different time of day, and so on. Really special treats are offered from the hand which is gradually presented closer and closer to the dog's mouth, and then a new bowl is introduced. Finally, the act of picking up the bowl is accomplished. Once the dog is comfortable with the movements around the bowl, the remaining changes are gradually faded out. The bowl is slowly placed back on the floor, the owner is no longer sitting with the dog but instead moves around the room, and finally, the dog is back in the kitchen for his meals.

Defending chew bones is usually a tougher problem to resolve because the aggression is often not triggered unless the dog actually "possesses" the bone. Once he has the bone, it is very difficult to do any form of desensitization or counterconditioning. In virtually all cases, I recommend the use of a head halter and a light line so the owner can block any aggressive responses. Then I recommend a procedure which gradually approximates possession of a bone: first, the owner holds it for the dog to chew, then it is held close to the floor so the dog can lay down, then it is held under the foot, and so on. The goal is to never provoke aggression - it is far better to go slowly and succeed than to move quickly and potentially fail.

There is no doubt that a phenomenon known as "dominance aggression" exists. It is not surprising. Dogs display dominance toward each other when they live together in a social group. We humans are certainly targets for all sorts of social behavior from dogs, including the nice behaviors of play, grooming, etc. So we can expect to also be the target of some nasty behavior. The difficulty I have is that dominance *displays* are common among groups of dogs living together but dominance *aggression* is not. Dogs rarely hurt each other. Maybe humans are less able to read the warning signs. Alternatively, I believe that dogs **learn** what behaviors produce good things. If baring my teeth and taking a bite out of my clients caused them to give me money, I probably would learn very quickly to do just that! A lot of what I see classified as dominance aggression is the dog who has learned to take advantage of the situation in which he finds himself. Dogs are extremely opportunistic. If they come across a good thing, they'll run with it. Sometimes, simply analyzing the situation in terms of what is in the best interest of the dog will allow you to see and change the contingencies rather than spending a great deal of time ignoring or crating a dog in the hope that he will adopt a more submissive attitude. Implementing a "work to earn" rule, while desensitizing and counterconditioning the dog to tolerate things he didn't before, such as being touched, picked up, or disturbed while sleeping, is often an effective treatment procedure. Sometimes, there is an element of defensive aggression thrown in and if the owner stops feeling like he has to dominate the dog, the dog won't feel like he is about to be attacked every few minutes by the owner and they can begin to develop a more friendly, cooperative relationship.

# Social Learning

I constantly get into arguments with people over whether dogs can imitate. Usually the argument degenerates into an argument of technicalities. This is because imitation is a precisely-defined form of social learning. Social learning involves any learning that occurs in a social context: a social group. A social group is at least two dogs together or at least one dog and one human. There are several distinct forms of social learning, of which imitation is one. I am not going to go through them all but if you want to read an excellent review, check out Whiten & Ham, 1992.

## Social Facilitation

Social facilitation refers to a process whereby one animal is motivated to engage in a particular behavior because someone else is doing it. Here's a good example. You're not at all hungry but for social reasons, you accompany your friend to a restaurant and once your friend's food arrives, you begin to feel a bit peckish and find yourself helping her to eat her food or ordering your own plate! Dogs do this all the time. One dog starts eating and they all want food. One dog starts drinking and suddenly everyone is thirsty. One dog starts barking and they all do. One dog attacks a prey animal or another dog and they all enter into the fray. I start making silly noises and Eejit joins in. A wolf on TV howls and suddenly Shaahiin is lifting his head to join the chorus. Sometimes dogs even try a novel food that they had previously rejected if another dog is ob-served to eat the food. A puppy learns to come in response to "come" because initially, this provides an opportunity to chase the adult dog. The effects of social facilitation is sometimes referred to as "pack behavior". Any species that gathers in social groups will engage in this type of learning.

Fears and phobias are often transmitted through social facilitation. I often get calls from people with a pair of very unfriendly dogs. The second dog was adopted in the hope that it would bring the first one around. Instead, they both went bad (the old rotten apple syndrome). This can be a serious concern for people who foster rescue dogs.

One of my all-time favorite studies was an investigation of a socially-facilitated phobia. A group of starlings were placed together in a cage. One single starling was caged right next to the group with only a mesh separating them so they could see each other and interact to some extent. The important point was that the group of birds could see into a compartment that the single bird could not. He had his own compartment in the same direction that he could see into. After the birds were settled and comfortable in this arrangement, an owl, which is a natural predators of starlings, was placed in the compartment to be viewed by the group of starlings. At exactly the same time, the compartment for the single starling was opened and it contained an innocuous Coca-Cola bottle. Upon sighting the owl, the group of starlings raised a horrible uproar, screaming and squawking in terrible fright. All the single starling could see was the pop bottle but obviously attributed all the fuss to this new thing it had never seen before. It started screaming and squawking as well and in one easy lesson, you have a starling that is plumb terrified of Coca-Cola bottles!

People socially transmit fears to their dogs via social facilitation all the time. Women who are wary of passing by men at night may quickly end up with a dog that barks ferociously at men. Handlers of guide dogs often have a hard time because if they are tentative when someone is following behind them or if they are afraid of loose dogs, the dog quickly develops the same fear and, sometimes, generalizes the fear to all strangers or all dogs. This sort of problem is extremely difficult to treat.

## Stimulus or Local Enhancement

Stimulus or local enhancement refers to a process where one animal is busy engaging in a behavior, which attracts the attention of another animal who moves closer to the first animal. Just by being in the right location or drawing attention to the appropriate stimulus, the second animal stumbles upon the same behavior through luck, happenstance, or social facilitation.

My favorite example of local enhancement, that *looks* for all the world like imitation, is the older dog that house trains the new puppy. In fact, the puppy tends to follow the older dog around and when the older dog goes to the correct spot to eliminate, the puppy accompanies him and lo and behold, all the smells elicit elimination in the puppy as well. Voila! The older dog has trained the puppy where to eliminate!

Local enhancement is likely the explanation for the dog that learns to heel by joining in with the trained dog. He can see that the trained dog is having a wonderful time being praised, fed, and played with in that spot right beside the handler. What an amazing place! Once the dog is there, following along to stay in the same spot, it is an easy thing for him to learn to sit, speed up, slow down, and turn. That's all heeling is, really - learning to stay right beside the handler.

A dog that has never dug in the yard before may be sparked into action if a visiting dog begins digging. The resident dog is attracted to the area and is exposed to stimuli that stimulate digging because of the behavior of the visiting dog. Then, even when the visiting dog is gone, the stimuli that trigger digging are still present and so he continues to dig on his own.

## Imitation

Strictly defined, imitation is the acquisition of an **entirely novel** behavior that is acquired solely by observing another animal engaging in the behavior. So, for instance, a dog watches another dog operate the flyball box and **later** (not at the same time or it could be a combination of social facilitation and local enhancement) when given access to his own flyball box, knows how to trigger it. To be sure the behavior is imitation and not local enhancement, you must also observe a dog that is able to investigate a flyball box, without having observed the dog demonstrating how it is triggered, *but did observe a dog getting a tennis ball from the box* (this ensures that the dog will be interested in checking out the box as a source of good things). If dogs that have not seen the demonstrator dog are not able to trigger the box as quickly and effectively as dogs that did see the demonstrator dog, then you would be fairly safe in saying that dogs are able to learn by imitation.

Having described that hypothetical experiment, let me conclude by saying there is virtually no evidence that animals, except for humans and the great apes (gorillas, orangutans, and chimpanzees), are capable of pure imitation. Some researchers have devoted their entire professional lives to devising ways to demonstrate imitation, without success. Sorry to rain on your parade, but dogs just don't seem to be able to manage learning by imitation.

# _Conclusion_

By now you have a reasonable understanding of how dogs learn and you should be in the position to think about and analyze your training procedures and practices. Dogs learn about stimuli, they learn about associations, and they learn about contingencies. They can learn with positive consequences, they can learn with negative consequences, and they can learn with a combination of positive and negative consequences. How a dog learns _best_ depends upon you and your personality, the dog and his personality, and what response you are attempting to teach. If this material has encouraged you to learn more about learning theory, I recommend that you enroll in Psychology courses at a nearby university. The Psychology department of any decent-sized university will offer courses covering learning theory, behavior modification, motivation, animal cognition, and comparative psychology. The Zoology department will also offer courses in ethology and animal behavior.

I hope this material will help you to

**_Excel-erate Your Dog's Learning!_**

# References and Recommended Readings

Animal Behavior Consultant Newsletter. Wright, J. & Borchelt,P (Editors). Department of Psychology, Mercer University, Macon GA 31207-0001.

Breland, K. & Breland, M. (1961). The misbehavior of organisms. *American Psychologist*, 61, 681-684.

Dobrzecka, C., Szwejkowska, G. & Konorski, J. (1966). Qualitative versus directional cues in two forms of differentiation. *Science*, 153, 87-89.

Domjan, M. (1993). *Domjan & Burkhard's The Principles of Learning and Behavior*. Brooks/Cole Publishing Company.

Domjan, M. (1996). *The Essentials of Conditioning and Learning*. Brooks/Cole Publishing Company.

Ellson, D. (1937). The acquisition of a token-reward habit in dogs. *Comparative Psychology*, 24, 505-517.

Kalish, H.L. (1981). *From Behavioral Science to Behavior Modification*. McGraw-Hill Book Company.

Mackintosh, N.J. (1974). *The Psychology of Animal Learning*. Academic Press.

Marder, A.R. & Voith, V. (1991). *Veterinary Clinics of North America: Small Animal Practice. Advances in Companion Animal Behavior*. W.B. Saunders Company.

Martin, G. & Pear, J. (1996). *Behavior Modification: What It Is and How To Do It*. Prentice Hall.

Polsky, R.H. (1995). *User's Guide to the Scientific and Clinical Literature on Dog and Cat Behavior.* Animal Behavior Counseling Services, Inc.

Pryor, K. (1984). *Don't Shoot the Dog: The New Art of Teaching and Training.* Bantam Books.

Romba, J. J. (1984). *Controlling Your Dog Away From You.* Abmor Press.

Schwartz, B. & Robbins, S.J. (1995). *Psychology of Learning and Behavior.* W. W. Norton & Company.

Shettleworth, S.J. Constraints on learning. *Advances in the Study of Behavior,* 4.

Skinner, B.F. (1951). How to teach animals. *Scientific American.*

Sundel, M. & Sundel, S.S. (1975). *Behavior Modification in the Human Services: A Systematic Introduction to Concepts and Applications.* John Wiley & Sons.

Tortora, D.F. (1983). Safety training: The elimination of avoidance-motivated aggression in dogs. *Journal of Experimental Psychology: General,* 112, 176-214.

Voith, V. L. & Borchelt, P. B. (1996). *Readings in Companion Animal Behavior.* Veterinary Learning Systems Co. Inc.

Whiten, A. & Ham, R. (1992). On the nature and evolution of imitation in the animal kingdom: Reappraisal of a century of research. *Advances in the Study of Behavior,* 21, 239-283.

Zbrozyna, A.W. (1983). Habituation of the threatening response in cats and kittens. *Acta Neurobiologie Experiments,* 43, 183-192.